To

Dr. Nirma

A friend, Mentor and Philosopher

with best compliments of

Mrinal and Dilip

2-19-2014.

So Smart But . . .

Allen Weiner

Foreword by Don Robert

JB JOSSEY-BASS

So Smart But . . .

How Intelligent People
Lose Credibility—
and How They Can Get It Back

BICENTENNIAL
1807
WILEY
2007
BICENTENNIAL

John Wiley & Sons, Inc.

Published by Jossey-Bass
A Wiley Imprint
989 Market Street, San Francisco, CA 94103-1741 www.josseybass.com

Readers should be aware that Internet Web sites offered as citations and/or sources for further information may have changed or disappeared between the time this was written and when it is read.

Jossey-Bass books and products are available through most bookstores. To contact Jossey-Bass directly call our Customer Care Department within the U.S. at 800-956-7739, outside the U.S. at 317-572-3986, or fax 317-572-4002.

Jossey-Bass also publishes its books in a variety of electronic formats. Some content that appears in print may not be available in electronic books.

Library of Congress Cataloging-in-Publication Data

Weiner, Allen, 1946-
    So smart but — : how intelligent people lose credibility—and how they can get it back / Allen Weiner ; foreword by Don Robert.
        p. cm.
    Includes bibliographical references.
    ISBN-13: 978-0-7879-8574-5 (cloth)
    ISBN-10: 0-7879-8574-0 (cloth)
        1. Communication in management. 2. Executive ability. 3. Performance. 4. Integrity. 5. Interpersonal communication. I. Title.
    HD30.3.W417 2007
    650.1—dc22   2006017860

Printed in the United States of America
FIRST EDITION
HB Printing   10 9 8 7 6 5 4 3 2

Contents

Foreword

I first met Allen Weiner four years ago under circumstances that are no doubt consistent with how he meets many of his clients for the first time. I had a major presentation looming on the not-so-distant horizon, and I was concerned about my ability to pull it off well. Sure, I had made dozens of speeches and presentations in the past, but this one felt a lot different to me.

I had joined Experian only a few months earlier and was unexpectedly asked to stand in for my boss, who had suddenly taken ill, at a global management conference. The conference was in a different country, and I was unfamiliar with the venue, the participants, and, truthfully, part of the subject matter. To make matters worse, the division of the company I was managing was underperforming, and I knew I had only limited time to come up with a plan to get things moving in the right direction. As if all this weren't enough, I had peeked at the attendee list for the conference, and I knew that our board and our global executive team would be well represented there—seeing me "in action" for the first time. There was no margin for error.

Allen came to my office for our first meeting. I expected he'd videotape me and give me some tips as to how I could better present my material to the audience. What I obtained from him that afternoon, however, was a lot more powerful.

He began our meeting by helping me understand the big picture—in other words, the *dimensions of credibility*. We talked about how a person should look and sound for maximum impact, the importance of listening well, and the art of thinking on one's feet.

What fascinated me about this whole discussion with Allen was that his approach was practical and scientific—backed up by research and test audience surveys. He told me *why* audiences responded to certain things and *why* they didn't respond to others. For example, I recall Allen's explaining to me that when a speaker starts out with a story and uses an introductory phrase like "You know, just the other day . . .," or "A couple of days ago I was chatting with Rick . . .," the impact on his audience is similar to that of an adult telling a child a "once upon a time" bedtime story. In other words, the audience, like the child, becomes attentive, relaxed, and receptive to the message. I was already hooked on Allen Weiner's ideas!

With Allen's help, I built a presentation I was proud to deliver at that big meeting. It was organized around his high-impact templates; delivered with punchy, meaningful words; and augmented by great visual aids. I was more confident as a communicator than I had ever been before because I had so many new tools at my disposal.

Throughout the course of my career, I have observed why people succeed or fail when it comes to getting promoted into key leadership positions. In the final analysis, domain expertise and the ability to execute seldom separate the winner and the loser—both of them usually already have those qualities. The people who make it to the top of their game, whatever that game might be, are the ones who have the ability to communicate with credibility—to senior management, to their own department, to the sales force, to their government regulators, to their board of directors, to legions of employees, or (most often) to their own boss.

Fortunately for all of us, Allen Weiner has finally put pencil to paper, and, in so doing, shared with all of us his unique, scientific understanding of the components of credibility. He has also given us the gift of many highly entertaining true-life stories and anecdotes that illustrate just how (to use his words) *intelligent people lose credibility—and how they can get it back.*

On the basis of my own continuing association with Allen, I can tell you firsthand that his very best, highest-impact ideas and

techniques are contained in this book. You will benefit tremen-
dously, for instance, by putting into practice Allen's advice on
improving your word choices, listening with credibility, and sounding likable.

Taking advantage of these tips alone could dramatically change
how you are perceived by others and have a positive impact on
your life.

I believe *So Smart But . . .* will take its place among the best
leadership training books of this decade, simply because so many
great things can happen when one learns to master the art of communicating with credibility. As you will see in this book, your job
as a communicator is to say things that listeners find interesting and
to hold their attention. If you learn to do that well, you'll love the
results. *So Smart But . . .* will put you on the course to do just that
and to enhance your chances of personal and career success!

Don Robert
CEO, Experian

Introduction

It was a snowy night in Chicago, late December 1996. Around eight o'clock, I was leaving a client's offices in the Hancock Building after a week of consulting. I knew a taxi was waiting on the curb to take me out to O'Hare and finally home to Los Angeles.

I walked slowly past a row of executive offices on my way to the lobby. The CEO occupied one of those offices. We had not spoken often after the engagement was arranged that past summer, but he saw me that night and motioned for me to come in to his office. He pointed toward one of the chairs facing his desk.

He was impressive. He had done a lot, and he had gotten other people to do a lot. Bankers, investors, and stockholders admired him. He was physically impressive, too: six foot four, perhaps fifty-eight years old.

I sat. We looked at each other for just a moment, and then he said, "You've been here for nearly seven months. Tell me something I don't know."

Every reader knows that consultants are supposed to be people who ask to borrow a client's wristwatch and then tell the client what time it is . . . and then keep the wristwatch.

That particular CEO was Mel Bergstein, chairman and CEO of DiamondCluster International. DiamondCluster is a management and advisory firm with six hundred consultants and a worldwide reach. Its teams have to collaborate with clients, and those teams live and die on their ability to build and hold credibility with client executives of every imaginable style.

I told Bergstein I had heard employee concerns about an important decision he was going to make. He sat back, thought about it, and said, "All right. That's new. Let me think about that."

I headed out to the taxi, settled in for the ride to O'Hare and thought, "Whew. Mel's as aware of the impact of his style as anyone I've worked with. If this nugget was new to him, I've been of some value."

I came back to my office and said to myself, "Every one of us should go into a consulting engagement prepared to answer that most fundamental of requests: 'Tell me something I don't know.' " Even though I had been in practice for twenty-one years, that night I became a made man, if "made man" means coming to grips with what we're paid to do: offer answers to the *big* questions.

So *Smart But . . .* intends to be the answer to your demand, "Tell me something I don't know." I would not be pleased if you, the reader, reacted to *So Smart But . . .* by saying, "It's common sense." Believe me, everything here should *make sense*, but it shouldn't be *common sense*. Common sense doesn't really add to anyone's storehouse of knowledge on a topic.

Why I've Titled This *So Smart But . . .*

Soon after our firm, Communication Development Associates (CDA), began as a corporate entity and began to get referral business, a call came from the office of the senior vice president of sales and marketing for one of America's largest retailers. He said, "I've got a potential client for you. His name is Dale. Dale knows retail at the subatomic level . . . at the particle level. But he can't communicate what he knows."

So many of the inquiries that come to CDA begin with a similar theme: "We have a number of executives who we're interested in placing in a professional development program. They've all been identified as high achievers. They are all incredibly bright. But they can't get their message across. They need help communicating."

What Communication Is
and What It Is Not

I need to explain here that many people who call a firm like ours think of communication skills as something that describes the way a person speaks or makes a presentation. If you look, for instance, at a performance review form at a typical Fortune 500 organization, you'll see Interpersonal Communication as one category and Leadership Competency as another. If an employee makes exceptionally good PowerPoint presentations, he or she might get an "Exceeds Expectations" under the category Interpersonal Communication. That phenomenon—that tendency for people to equate good presentations with "good communicator"—deserves some attention. And I'm going to address it. But the point I need to make right here is that *all* the leadership competencies require communication skill to come alive. For instance, take a line item under Leadership Competency that reads "Champions our vision." One way to show that you've championed the vision is to talk about the company's vision in an inspiring way.

The Five Factors of Credibility
(or the Original Recipe)

Scholars first identified *source credibility* as an important variable in the communication equation in the 1960s. People wanted to know if the source of a message could control some of the factors that would make him or her believable. Aristotle called this notion, this emphasis on the source of a message, *ethos, the source's most potent means of persuasion.* Dr. James McCroskey and other researchers carried on a systematic analysis of source credibility through the 1960s, 1970s, and 1980s (McCroskey, 1966; Applebaum & Anatol, 1973; Bandhuim & Davis, 1972; Berlo, Lemert, & Mertz, 1971; Falcione, 1974; McCroskey, Hamilton, & Weiner, 1973; McCroskey & Jensen, 1975; McCroskey & Young, 1981).

McCroskey demonstrated empirically, through study after study, that a communicator had to demonstrate five qualities in order to be experienced as totally credible. Those five qualities are

- Competence
- Character
- Composure
- Sociability
- Extroversion

McCroskey was one of the scholars who came to West Virginia University in 1973, and I studied under him. I continue to monitor his academic research on credibility to be certain that the model holds true. Over the past thirty years, we've used our seminars as focus groups to substantiate McCroskey's early findings in a non-laboratory setting.

Recently he forwarded an article with recent research updates (McCroskey & Teven, 1999). He writes that a separate credibility factor, *goodwill,* or "the intent toward the receiver of the message," has become a "lost dimension," that it's been ignored. Goodwill could be seen as a sixth independent factor that leaders should think about as they communicate. I will return to goodwill with special emphasis in Chapter Nine when we cover management styles and compliance issues, but here is a teaser:

Goodwill, or perceived caring, is seen as a means of opening communication channels more widely. McCroskey suggests that three elements may result in a person's being seen as more caring: understanding, empathy, and responsiveness.

Understanding is knowing another person's ideas, feelings, and needs. A person with understanding seems to know what we're talking about, what we're thinking. Others seem to be less sensitive to our communication. They don't recognize when our feelings are hurt, when we have a problem, when we need their help.

Empathy, in McCroskey's view, is one person's identification with another person's feelings. This means that the person not only understands the other's views but accepts them as valid, even if he or she does not agree with those views.

Responsiveness involves a person's acknowledging another person's attempt to communicate. We judge responsiveness by how quickly someone reacts to our communication, how attentive he or she is to us. If we perceive a person as being responsive, we feel that he or she cares. So that's the teaser. But for my current purposes, let's return to the "Big Five, Original Recipe" factors.

The original five credibility factors, prior to the "discovery" of goodwill, were considered independent of each other and together able to explain the entire notion. In other words, they were "MECE": mutually exclusive and collectively exhaustive.

Distinguishing Communication from Credibility

From the beginning of my practice, I have told clients that any particular communication behavior is simply a tactic and that achieving credibility is the strategy. In other words, a beautifully said simple sentence is a tactic. The degree to which you speak that way helps achieve the strategy of coming across credibly. Or if people feel that you would be more effective if you answered questions more concisely, you can master the tactic of speaking concisely fairly easily. And if through your ability to give concise answers people perceive you as able to take a complex issue and simplify it, you are coming across to them as a very competent person. And now we're talking about one of the five keys to credibility.

The title of this book, *So Smart But . . .* , is intended to convey that for our firm, "smart" clients are a given. I've always said to my wife, "No one works with smarter people than we do if you believe the descriptions you hear from their colleagues."

"Jane is a technical genius, but . . ."

"John is incredibly talented, but . . ."

"Tony is a very bright guy, but . . ."

"Cory's been in the business since start-up and knows it
  backwards and forwards, but . . ."

I'm terrifically relieved to know that our clients are considered
to be so smart. First of all, it's highly rewarding to be around smart
people. And second, no amount of really neat tips can add IQ
points to a client's profile. We've worked with scientists in aero-
space; medical doctors and professionals in pharmaceuticals
research; financial wizards in investment banking; business whiz
kids at the world's largest consulting firms; incredibly talented sales
and marketing executives in hundreds of commercial products; and
engineers at some of the world's largest oil and gas companies. Even
though all of them have been recognized for their talent, all of them
have also been described as having something to work on . . . the
"but" that acts like the noisy tin cans dragging behind the car of a
newly married couple.

Credibility and the Performance Review

A thorough review of all the thousands of corporate performance
review forms reveals that McCroskey's five keys to credibility are
accurate. That is, all the qualities on which employees are evaluated fall into one of the five credibility "buckets"—I am going to
base *So Smart But . . .* on these factors. And let me say here that,
over the years, I took the liberty of renaming "sociability" to "likability" and "extroversion" to "high energy." I simply had too many
clients asking me to explain the meaning of the original labels.

But first, read through this list of a few qualities included on a
performance review form I've chosen from our files. I'm going to list
a review line item and suggest the credibility bucket it falls into.

Manages workforce performance	Composure
Appropriately delegates	Composure
Builds a high-performance organization	Competence

Demonstrates individual leadership skills	All five
Passionately drives our strategy	Extroversion (high energy)
Fosters a climate of innovation	Character
Fosters and models our values	Character
Champions our vision	Competence
Engages in innovation	Competence
Focuses on performance and results	Competence
Demonstrates interpersonal skills	Sociability (likability)

These are just a few I picked at random. Look at your own performance review form, and you will see that you are measured against the oldest, truest, most authentic measures of your performance: the five factors of credibility.

Credibility and 360° Feedback

360° feedback instruments have been around since the early 1980s. They allow your colleagues to give opinions about your performance. These instruments were given the shorthand title 360° to symbolize collecting feedback from around the compass points. That is, you are seeking feedback from those senior to you, your peers, your direct reports, and your customers if applicable. Most feedback forms are distributed one time and one time only in a given year. Some of them have nearly one hundred line items for a feedback giver to consider. Most are the result of long periods of needs analysis of the entire corporation by internal HR professional development experts. The forms have the outward appearance and sense of importance you would expect from the company's corporate charter. But, once again, they reflect five and only five qualities: competence, composure, character, sociability, and extroversion. Why don't 360° feedback instruments simply ask feedback providers these five questions?

1. Am I competent at my job? (competence)
2. Do I come across as having things under control? (composure)
3. Do I show respect for you? (character)
4. Am I a team player? (sociability)
5. Do I show energy and drive? (extroversion)

Notice that I've used some new language in these five questions. For instance, I used the word "respect" in question 3 on character. I'm going to talk about these terms as each chapter rolls out.

Here again are some random samples of 360° feedback instrument questions:

Do I thoroughly understand my duties?

Am I a self-starter?

Am I an expert in my field?

Do I take the initiative to do extra work and volunteer for new assignments?

The first and third questions tap competence. The second and fourth tap extroversion. As I've said, McCroskey's labels are going to come in for a lot of discussion in *So Smart But . . .* The point here, however, is that his original framework, and even more so now that he's added the concept of "goodwill," is collectively exhaustive. There ain't no more. That's all there is. And thank goodness for that, because it clarifies what all of us need to do to be credible.

In Chapter Ten, I will show you precisely how you can use www.essessnet.com to measure your credibility. You can assess yourself and see how your assessment compares with others' perceptions of you. You might want to fasten your seat belt when that time comes. U.S. presidents use tracking polls to follow their credibility ratings throughout their term. You should be able to do the same thing . . . and you can.

So Smart But . . .

1

THE LOOK AND SOUND
OF CREDIBILITY

Nicole is a star. Everyone says so. She's very nearly at the top of her game and only forty years old. She's married to a great guy, and they have two kids. I know just how highly she is regarded by the CEO. But her story wasn't always this upbeat. Eight years ago she nearly blew it. She's spent the last few years digging herself out of a huge credibility crater. What did she do that was so bad?

Nicole and her husband had decided they didn't want a houseful of "things." They wanted a simpler life. But their desire for a simpler life and the reality of life crashed into each other when she was promoted to vice president and her company gave her a very generous gift: a John Lennon original lithograph from a very exclusive Fifth Avenue gallery. Nicole decided to return the lithograph and take the cash.

The gallery owner gave Nicole the cash value and then called the person who had put the order in to let her know that the receiver wanted cash. The gallery owner thought the purchaser of such a gift should know. Unfortunately, that person was the wife of the biggest original investor in Nicole's company. It didn't seem right to her that Nicole should be returning what was felt to be a personal gift . . . a *very* personal gift. The investor's wife was miffed. She was a traditionalist from the old school. One simply didn't return a gift like that. News of her displeasure was passed on to the CFO, who passed it on to the CEO. What started as a desire to simplify her life ended up complicating Nicole's ambitions. The buyer thought she was ungrateful and just plain stupid.

Nicole asked me one day, "Do you think I need to do something about this? Will this hurt my career?" I told her to go back to the gallery, reacquire the lithograph, and write a note explaining why she'd returned it. The note she wrote said, "I wasn't raised to appreciate fine art. Growing up, our family saw fine art as something for people who had more education and, frankly, more money. I think that's why I've felt a little uncomfortable aspiring to own art and a little embarrassed at the thought of accepting something like that as a gift. I thought my parents would point to this piece on my wall as perhaps 'forgetting where I came from.' Please forgive my thoughtlessness." That note helped Nicole get back on track.

I told Nicole that some people would call what she did a mistake. Some would say she just didn't use common sense. Some would say she showed a lack of EQ. Some police officers might have seen her leaving the shop and said, "She looks kind of hinky."

People Pick Up on the Most Subtle Body Motions

Why "hinky"? A few years ago I taught communication programs with police officers from the Los Angeles Police Department and the Los Angeles County Sheriff's Department. One night I heard them use the word "hinky," as in "He looked hinky." The officers agreed that after you've gained a certain amount of experience on the job, you get a feeling, a feeling you can't put your finger on, that someone is not acting right, not driving right, not walking right. They call that hinky. The feeling comes from a well-developed ability to read nonverbal communication, or body language. (By the way, one of the officers told me that a person who touches his or her face while answering an officer's questions is probably just nervous and probably not lying. A liar, he argued, gets pretty good at controlling nervous tics. A truth teller is simply nervous at finding herself in a situation with a police officer and shows it by touching or scratching her face.)

In *Human Communication* (Burgoon, Hunsaker, & Dawson, 1994), the authors repeat a notion I had heard many times in class:

[Sixty] percent of the social meaning in interpersonal interchange is transmitted nonverbally. When someone says, 'I could tell from his

eyes that he was angry' or 'Her voice made it clear that we were finished talking,' he or she is actually responding to nonverbal communication. Adults also give great weight to nonverbal cues when
verbal and nonverbal messages are contradictory. Imagine talking to
a friend who insists she is not angry yet her lips are pursed and she
moves away every time you try to get close to her. Are you likely to
believe her words or her actions?

Once my original partners and I began professional practice, we
heard clients described in simple terms like these:

"He looks arrogant."

"He looks smart."

"He looks confident."

"She looks friendly."

"She looks energetic."

"He looks decisive."

"He looks credible."

Think about the phrase, "He looks smart." So simple sounding,
but how does one reach such a conclusion? Is it the clothes? Is it the
grooming? Is it the glasses? Is it the high forehead? Is it the facial
expression he makes when he's listening?

Now we also heard these phrases:

"He sounds arrogant."

"He sounds smart."

"He sounds confident."

"She sounds friendly."

"She sounds energetic."

"He sounds decisive."

"He sounds credible."

Think about the statement, "He sounds smart." Is it the numbers he quotes? Is it the "big words" he uses? Is it the absence of "uhhh" and "ummm"?

When my son was a baby, now and then a stranger would say, "Your baby is so smart." How would anyone know a baby was smart? It could have been the way he pronounced his baby talk. If baby talk is clear, that baby will be called a smart baby. Maybe instead of "Da Da" he said, "Dr. Dada." Now it might have been his facial expression. He might have been unusually alert looking. (Matt, can you forgive me for using you as an example?) And it remains that way through life. Someone who is "well spoken" will be thought smart.

We noticed that people who described our clients were just as quick to say "She looks credible" as they were to say "She sounds credible." Interestingly enough, they were not as quick to say "She uses words that show credibility." Figure 1.1 sums up our discoveries about perception based on body language or based on the way someone sounded.

It is very important that I affirm the meaning of this little pie chart. I am not suggesting that only 10 percent of your message and its meaning comes through in your content. I am suggesting that only 10 percent of the *criticism* of your message is tied directly to the

Figure 1.1. Credibility Doesn't Depend on Word Choice.

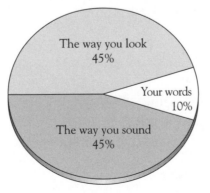

choice of one word versus another. There are exceptions, as you will read here, but those only serve to highlight the rule.

Some of us are visually oriented and clearly pay more attention to the way our colleagues look. Actually, I would rather put it this way: some of us have an eye for things. You might have an eye for graphic design, for instance. Others are more aware of the aural. They focus more on the way their colleagues sound. Or, to put it in the same terms, they have an ear for things, just as one might have an ear for music. Please note, though, that even if some of us are visually oriented, it's easy to get focused on the way someone sounds if it really sticks out—and vice versa.

I am vaguely suspicious of the idea that students ought to be taught in a way that caters to their learning preference. I think the teacher in us should be clever in the way we explain things so that we delight our listener's eyes *and* ears. And we certainly should be able to explain something without resorting to PowerPoint. Can you imagine the look on my wife's face if I were to say, "Let's talk about where we're going to come up with the money for College X versus College Y. I know you are a 'visual learner,' so I've set up a presentation in the dining room." She would think I had drunk the Kool-Aid. Believe me, she would pick up from the look on my face and the sound of my voice that I have concerns. A visual person could still say, "You sounded serious." An aural person would still say, "You painted a pretty clear picture for me."

If a speaker has a lot of vocal tics, such as the aforementioned "ummms" and "uhhhs," any of us, including visually oriented people, might begin to focus on that. Even if we tend to pay more attention to the way someone sounds, we would still be likely to get distracted by the look on that person's face when he or she is answering questions. One quality or another is always the subject of intense focus while other qualities remain hazy or unfocused.

All of us would like to control what everyone else focuses on. No doubt most of us would prefer that people pay attention to our message and not be distracted by the way we look or sound.

I once heard a poet talking about the impact of a reader noticing an error, spelling or otherwise, in a poem. He said, "It brings you to the surface." You realize that he wants his reader to be immersed in the work. It's troubling to the poet if you notice some mistake that snaps you out of that depth and brings you back to mundane reality. The same thing can be said of a presenter or conversationalist in a meeting. Whether it's "uhhhs" or a mispronounced word in a speech, it takes the listener out of the flow of things and "brings him to the surface."

As each chapter of *So Smart But . . .* unfolds, you will see that my suggestions will focus either on a behavior that will make you *look* credible or one that will make you *sound* credible. I'll have tips on the words you should use too. But, again, thinking back to the pie chart, you need to remember that generally speaking, you are not judged for the specific words you choose as much as you are for the way you look or the way you sound. The totality of the message— the way it is organized and expressed—is critical. But the choice of, say, "good" instead of "great" is not worth the time and effort communicators put into thinking about it. Please keep in mind that I am not talking about words that reflect poor grammar. Those count. You will read about one such mistake (of mine) in the section after next.

The Way You Look

Researchers have studied seven separate categories related to how you look. Your perceived credibility can be affected by any one of them. You'll be surprised to see that there is a lot more to this than simply the way you dress. Here are the categories and little comments we've heard about each one of them.

1. The way you use personal space—proxemics. "She stands too close to me."

2. The way you touch others—haptics. "He has a weak handshake."

3. The way you use time—chronemics. "She's never late with a deliverable."

4. Your facial expression—oculesics. "If you're feeling happy, tell your face."

5. The way you move your body—kinesics. "His posture was very relaxed."

6. The way you dress, the way you groom yourself, *and* your body size—physical appearance. "The fact that he's so overweight tells me his life in not in balance."

7. The way you decorate your space—artifacts. "Her office is so obsessively organized that she must not have time for real work."

Some of my clients think that anyone who would judge them based solely on how they look must be vapid and shallow. Maybe so, but it's simply human nature to be distracted by such things. I've often said to seminar participants, "If you have a message that is very, very, very compelling, people will not be distracted by the way you look. But if your message is just so-so, you are opening yourself up to these kinds of distractions. A compelling message, delivered in a compelling way, will be immune to distraction." How do you make your message compelling and credible? That question is answered in this book.

The Way You Sound

A few years ago, in a piece of performance feedback I received after a seminar, someone said, "Whatever happened to the verb, 'to say'? You, Dr. Weiner, used 'to go' instead of properly using 'to say.' To quote you, you said, 'I told the man that he should speak with more energy, and he goes, "It was as energetic as I can be."' You are a communication consultant and should know better!" Of course, he was right. And he is proof that the things you say, the seemingly smallest errors, can dramatically alter someone's perception of your credibility.

We have studied twelve categories related to how you sound:

1. The volume of your voice. "He sounds meek."
2. The tone of your voice. "She was dripping with sarcasm."
3. The speed of your voice. "He sounded tired."
4. The length of your sentences. "She sounded indecisive."
5. Your grammar. "He sounded uneducated. Send the next candidate in."
6. Your accent. "She sounds so intelligent. Let's give her the offer."
7. Your vocabulary. "He has to tailor his message to his audience."
8. Your pronunciation. "Why does she keep saying 'orientated'? It's 'oriented.' She's not well read."
9. Your logic. "I couldn't follow his train of thought. He sounds totally lost."
10. Your data. "We'll need better data than that! He sounds unprepared."
11. Your syntax. "Boy. Just one simple sentence now and then would be so nice. She's way too detailed."
12. Your little vocal tics. "He was, uhhh, clearly, uhhh, nervous."

It can be daunting to realize how many behaviors your listeners can pick up on, behaviors they have an ear for. If you're lucky, your listener might forgive your speaking idiosyncrasies. But you may be in a situation where a listener catches every nuance, just as my listener called me on the wrong verb. Good luck.

You Cannot Not Communicate

The folks who think about you and your communication style—your boss, your peers, your direct reports, your clients and customers, your significant others and children, your friends—don't quit watching when you stop talking. You are under the microscope when you listen, when you walk, and when you sit. I remember my father admonishing me once after watching me with my toddler: "Don't worry about whether he's listening to you. Just remember that he is always watching you." Although "You cannot not communicate" is a phrase attributed to Dr. Paul Watzlawick, a very famous psychotherapist who taught at Stanford University, my dad, Hyman Weiner the haberdasher, got it right too.

So now we add another factor to the credibility equation. People are evaluating how you look and how you sound not only when you are *talking* but also when you are *listening*. If we express this idea in the form of a matrix, it looks like Figure 1.2.

Say, for instance, that you conduct a 360° feedback for a subordinate. When it comes back to her, your subordinate reads that she can be closed-minded once she has arrived at her point of view. She reads that she is not open to the views of others. She reads that some people think that, while she is listening, it is clear that she is formulating her response.

When it is time for you to go over the feedback with her, she says to you, "Can you give me some input on what I am doing that makes people feel this way?" You could show her a filled-in version of the matrix, as shown in Figure 1.3.

Your subordinate says, "So I give off this closed-minded vibe even when I'm not saying a thing?" You would say, "Yes. It comes

Figure 1.2. You're Always Projecting Impressions.

	How you look	How you sound
While talking		
While listening		

Figure 1.3. Examples of Projecting Impressions.

	How you look	How you sound
While talking	Very little animation. No eye contact. Dismissive hand gestures.	Clipped speech. Abrupt speech. No-nonsense language.
While listening	Head stock still. No body movement.	Total silence. Abrupt answers.

through in your body language and in the abruptness of your answers to people's questions. It is having an impact on your credibility."

So Smart and So SMART

As a student, I loved reading and doing studies about the behavior of a source, or sender, of a message. I also loved the research about the message itself. How does the source look and sound? How does the message look and sound? But as they used to say in advertisements for the Ginsu Knife, "But wait! That's not all!"

There are actually five interesting ways to study credibility. In addition to the source (S) and the message (M), you can investigate the arena (A) where communication takes place. You can look at the nature of the receivers (R) of the message and whether you are targeting the right ones in the first place. Finally, you can look at the timing (T) of the action. (Haven't you heard people say, for instance, that feedback should be given to a person as soon as possible after the behavior? That's a timing issue.) Put all five of these elements together, and you get a great acronym to start your journey: SMART.

Suppose, for example, that you've received some feedback saying that you've lost your colleague's trust. Take out a pen, draw a little chart along the lines of Figure 1.4, and think through the problem using SMART to assess your credibility.

Figure 1.4.   Evaluating a Loss of Trust.

Style	Is my body language sending the wrong signal?
Message	Did I say something that sounded disingenuous?
Arena	Did I speak up in the wrong place?
Receiver	Did I pick the wrong person to share something with?
Timing	Did I speak up at the wrong time?

So many clients have asked me how to further develop their sense of sight for the way they, and others, look or their sense of hearing for the way they and others sound. I tell them, "Keep your ears open for the way novel writers create messages for their characters in a novel and your eyes open for the way actors eventually portrayed those characters." You're going to read some great examples right here in *So Smart But . . .*

2

SO SMART, BUT CAN'T TAILOR THE MESSAGE TO THE AUDIENCE

In the Introduction, I mentioned Dale: "Dale knows retail at the subatomic level . . . at the particle level. But he can't communicate what he knows." Dale represents millions of workers around the world who have accumulated a vast amount of knowledge about their area of expertise.

As I wrote in the Introduction, *So Smart, But . . .* describes and advises you about behavior based on the original dimensions of credibility: competence, composure, character, likeability, and high energy. Competence is generally a given. That explains the "so smart" in the title. But technical competence alone doesn't account for the entire dimension. Your ability to explain concepts with messages that resonate with listeners, and furthermore, your ability to alter your approach depending on various listener factors, also contributes to perceptions that you are competent.

In this chapter, I will describe, explain, and advise you on the skill you need to translate your intellect into messages that resonate with management. As you might imagine, the overwhelming number of suggestions are going to be about the way you should *sound* while *talking*. (Can someone *look* too technical while talking? Yes. Keep those pen protectors out of your shirt pocket.)

Before we go any further, I need to talk about something I just said: "into messages that resonate with management." Doubts about your credibility can come from anyone, but I have a bias toward counseling clients who are suffering doubts from their management, because the consequences are most profound when management doubts an employee's credibility. Even if your credibility is at risk with the people who report to you, or at risk with your peers, you will feel the consequences most directly when your management gets wind of credibility problems and embraces them.

Management's perceptions about your ability to "tailor" grow out of hearing you present as well as hearing you answer their questions about what you've presented. Some of my clients are better tailors in the original presentation. Maybe it's because they've had a chance to think through what they want to say. That's not a sure thing, but it may help. Other clients are better at the give and take of spontaneous question and answer. In any case, good tailors are great at both.

Tailoring Your Message Before the Questions Start

A few weeks ago, after a client meeting I ran into Dan, my client's (Adam) boss at the elevator. Here's the backstory. Adam's boss, Dan, suggested to him that he work with me as a way of addressing some issues that they had talked about in Adam's annual performance review. Dan told Adam at the review that he felt Adam didn't take things seriously, that he was too impulsive in decision making, and that he was dismissive of Dan's way of thinking on various business issues. Dan called me shortly after the review to get me prepared for my eventual meetings with Adam. (I always call this the "work order.") My plan for the engagement included getting Adam to come across as more open to his boss's point of view and more thorough in the way he argued his own points of view. In the early meetings, I focused on tailoring the message before the questions started.

The first meeting with Adam went well. I thought I had my finger on the "fix." But after talking with Dan in the elevator on the way out of the building, it jumped out at me that one of the reasons Dan felt that Adam was "casual" was Dan's perception that a more thorough argument implies a more "formal" approach. He said, "Adam is way too casual on issues that justify a more formal analysis." By a more formal analysis, he meant an analysis that proves that one has thought through all the facets of the issue before coming to a conclusion. In other words, getting to the point too quickly may make someone's presentation easy to understand but can imply that he or she has ignored important facts. Subsequently Adam communicated with this greater degree of "formality." So far, so good.

A few weeks later, once again generally pleased with my third meeting with Adam, I heard evidence that Dan equated familiarity with arcane detail with "genius." I ran into him on the way out of the building again, and he reminded me that we had initially met a year ago. I said, "No way. I would've guessed it was a few months ago." He said, "You know, I have a friend who can remember what he wore on a given day and what he ate on a given day. The guy's a genius!"

Now what does that say to you? It said to me that Adam's boss associates a good memory of certain facts with brainpower, with intellect, with genius. Adam also told me that one of his peers takes very careful notes in meetings and that Dan looks positively at that. In the boss's eyes, Adam's neglect of little details not only shows that he's not a genius but also shows that he's dismissive of someone who does. Adam, hearing my take on this, said, "The little details drive me nuts, but I'll work harder at giving them to Dan."

That story illustrates credibility problems arising out of the original message. It goes to the heart of this chapter. How do you calibrate the right level of detail in the original message? Adam's lucky that Dan was reasonably clear in telling him what he wanted in order to improve their relationship. It's not always that way.

I've been giving clients a handout this past year, a graphic that "spells out" for them why their boss might want them to participate in one of our seminars or receive coaching with us. I think of it as a senior management wish list; it will give you a sense of management's primary concerns about the way their direct reports regularly communicate. I prepared this list because of a conversation with a client. After this client and I had been working together for a month—and this comes after a heart-to-heart with his boss about the need to improve the way he comes across if he aspired for promotion—a colleague asked this client why he was meeting with me. He said, "I'm not sure. It has something to do with the way I communicate." The colleague told me about that conversation. Well, I was disappointed, to say the least, in my own ability to express to the client why we were working together.

Senior Management's Wish List

- Fewer wasted words
- Much more direct
- Ability to simplify complex ideas
- More ideas to enhance revenue or reduce waste
- Better interpretations of what you see
- More observable energy
- Better at forming relationships
- Doing things much faster

- A more respectful listener
- A quicker thinker
- More confidence
- A better writer
- Better at seeing what's going on
- More time spent on things that get the ball down the field
- Reacting faster to requests

Can you see how many of them reflect management's desire for you to show your credibility by learning how to be more direct and succinct and to the point? And how many of them show a desire for you to know the difference between the really important considerations and the mildly important ones? And how many express a desire for all of us to be more "big picture"?

Figure 2.1 is a facsimile of a bull's-eye graphic I hand out to clients to communicate what they should focus on in their work with me. In the center to emphasize its importance is management's wish list, the middle zone represents the client's personal wish list, and the outer zone represents what I want for the client. My wish list has only one wish: that the client get promoted. The target includes what I want for the client because in my work with him or her, I might see things that neither management nor the client recognize as behavior that has an impact on the client's chance of promotion.

Figure 2.1. What Should You Work On?

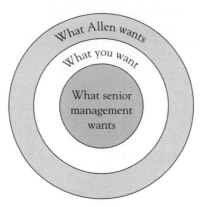

Main Point, Breadth, Depth, Height, and Sight: An Overview

You have five possible ways to express yourself on a topic. One, you can simply *make your point*. Two, you can describe the *breadth* of your thinking around that point. Three, you can go into *depth* or detail about your point. Four, you can elevate the implications of your point or express what's called *height*. And five, you can show your vision about your point with *sight*. By sight, I'm talking about predictions you can make (optimistic ones, we hope) about the issue. Figure 2.2 is a diagram of these five ways.

Obviously you could express a complex message about a topic that includes all the five parts. But my intention is for you to understand how to contribute your thoughts on any topic by skillfully picking and choosing among the five. In that way, your colleagues will hear you as capable of detail when necessary and capable of expressing only the "big picture" when necessary. That is, if you are in fifty meetings this year, I want you to be able to show your talent across all five ways so that, behind your back, people will say, "She not only gets to the point on that topic but also knows the breadth, depth, and strategic implications of it. And she shows great vision about it too."

Earlier I described a call about a technical person who was perceived by her "executive committee" as unable to shift gears from

Figure 2.2. The Five Ways You Project Your Intellect.

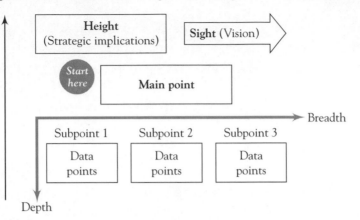

details to broad strokes. By executive committee, I'm referring to a select group of executives, sometimes called the "leadership team," who some clients get face time with if they're lucky. More common is a committee's admonition to "wait until we ask for details." The core of Figure 2.2 should help you see how that works in practical terms.

Main Point

Do you see where I've indicated the message's starting point in Figure 2.2? The box simply says Main Point. Picture yourself at a meeting. Someone says, "The next item on the agenda is the overseas facility. Who wants to start?" You clear your throat and say, "I think we should do it." That's your main point. Clear as a bell. Succinct. And, by the way, there's no problem in using the word "think." This is an example of a word whose use has very little to do with the overall impact of the message and your overall credibility. After all, everyone wants to know what you think. Isn't it funny that no one criticizes the questioner for asking, "What do you think?" but so many people ask me if it sounds indecisive to say, "Here's what I think" instead of something like, "I'm absolutely sure we should do it." (Maybe the questioners should ask, "What do you absolutely know?")

Breadth

Your understanding of the breadth of an issue is reflected in all the reasons you feel the way you do about it. In Figure 2.2, you can see three boxes in the middle labeled Subpoint 1, Subpoint 2, and Subpoint 3.

My favorite way of explaining breadth is to remind you of the cliché "Faster, Better, Cheaper." I'm going to be adding more to the notion of breadth later. But for the time being, these three serve to make the point. Here is a case where a cliché makes a lot of sense. Each term offers so much content on its own, and the three together paint a vivid picture about the value of the entire proposition. They show your listeners a tremendous breadth of thinking.

If someone were to ask a technical person to prepare a presentation on the reasons for moving forward with a new technology, the presenter could say, "It's faster, better, and cheaper. We can get twice as much done in half the time. It's a smarter product that simplifies the whole process for users, and it's an incredible deal for all it delivers."

The implication here is that even though the presenter is technical, he or she is not focused *entirely* on technological benefits. He or she shows a grasp of financial implications and understands the value of saving time.

At CDA, we've suggested an additional five pieces to the breadth puzzle. Along with "faster, better, and cheaper," they are meant to be used and switched at will depending on the information you are presenting. Figure 2.3 illustrates both the positive and negative versions of the eight parts.

When you think about it, an attempt to change someone's attitude in your direction generally asks him or her to change from their current thinking, the status quo, to your thinking: a change in the status quo. They, however, can try to make a case for the status quo. You'll say, "What I'm suggesting is faster, better, and cheaper." They'll respond, "No, it's not. It's slower, worse, and more expensive." Figure 2.3 gives you a sense of how you would argue

Figure 2.3. The Eight Parts to Breadth.

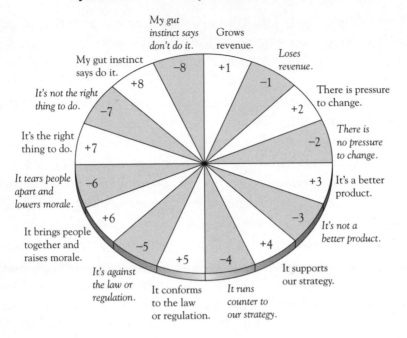

for something as well as how you'd argue *against* it. But keep this in mind: many listeners, more than you might think, have an instinct toward rejecting out of hand your prediction that something negative will happen. It's called a "fear appeal." A politician, for instance, could tell us that pulling troops out of a war zone will create more problems. That's a fear appeal. In other words, "things will get worse." Or she could say, alternatively, that keeping our troops in a war zone will keep things under control and create more stability. "Things will get better." She's predicting a positive outcome. Most listeners' attitudes are swayed with a positive prediction.

If our speaker on new technology were to use all eight, she might say, "This purchase makes sense because one, it's going to be so much faster. Two, it's simpler. Three, it will save us a lot of money—there's a real revenue upside. Four, it supports our strategy. Five, it has passed the legal department's review. Six, it will raise the morale of the entire workforce. Seven, we've followed our ethical standards in bidding it out. Finally, I have twenty years of experience in this area, and everything tells me it will be successful."

Do not use all eight at one time unless you're preparing a written document on the subject. But you get the idea, right? Become familiar with all eight.

Depth

If you listen to the questions that all of us are asked at work, you can easily tell the difference between those that seek the breadth of your knowledge and those that seek depth. The following are breadth questions: "What's the problem?" "Why do you feel that way?" "What's the value?" "Why are you hesitant?" In contrast, depth questions seek very specific information, such as the following:

"Who on their end needs to sign off?"

"How much did we spend on this last year?"

"How many subscribers do we need?"

"How many scholarships did we offer in 2001?"

"How long has he been their national sales manager?"

"How do you measure the value?"

"What are the metrics?"

Our research and experience reveals that listeners consider two types of information to be legitimate details or signs of depth: (1) an ease of manner with names, dates, and numbers; and (2) a memory for conversations with important players. If you say, "The new technology is much faster," you would follow that with words like, "In successive rounds of testing, we saved three man-hours per cycle. I have some information here about how the testing was done." If you followed that with, "It's also much simpler to use," you might then say, "I was talking to Ron Smithers in Finance yesterday. He told me he's never found an application as simple to use as this one. He said it would mean a lot less stress to his entire department."

Height

I met recently with David, a pharmaceutical salesman back East. His boss, Tom, referred him to us for executive coaching. Tom told me that there was no account David couldn't handle and handle well. He also said that there was some question about David's appropriateness for a regional manager position because some people felt that he could not or would not "raise the level of discussion to thirty thousand feet." When David and I met, he repeated this. He said he had been told about "the thirty thousand feet thing" and didn't understand why anyone would feel that way.

This particular case concerns a fellow who is not perceived as overly technical. But it is a good one to use as an example because it demonstrates a failure to demonstrate what we call *height*, or the strategic view.

Your ability to communicate height—your view of the landscape, your view when you get up on the balcony and look down at events—is of immeasurable value to your colleagues. Because my firm works with smart people, we assume that they are capable of seeing the bigger picture. They do not, however, always communicate what they see.

The simplest, easiest way for you to demonstrate an eye for height is to introduce your thoughts with words like, "Here's what I see when I helicopter up." There are a number of phrases that executives use to introduce such thinking. And the phrases, by the way, are important because they serve as signposts. Remember, it doesn't matter exactly what those words are. It's the use of a signpost that is important. Signposts tell the listener, "Stop here for a moment because I am about to take you in a new direction." Here are some more:

"Let's get up on the balcony for a moment and look at this from the broader perspective."

"Those are the details. Here are some larger issues."

"As this goes forward, we'll need to be asking ourselves some questions." (And while I'm on this, many executives have told me anecdotally that a colleague who raises questions during the height piece brings credibility to his or her message.)

"While this appears at first glance to be about customer service, at a higher level it's about our survival as a major player in this market."

David was always more than capable of seeing the larger picture. Now he can speak to it.

Sight

George Herbert Walker Bush suffered the pundit perception of not having vision. "He doesn't have the 'vision thing.' " Bush called attention to it himself, revealing his possibly cynical doubt about the very idea. But it would have been harder for Dana Carvey of *Saturday Night Live* to impersonate the president saying "Here's where I see things next year," than the phrase he did repeat often, "We need to be prudent." Our company has been asking executives about this issue for thirty years. Their answers and our own observations lead us to believe that vision is another quality that our clients have but do not always communicate.

What does it take to show your raw intellectual bandwidth *and* your vision? How can you show that you can see over the horizon to a better day? One, you have to predict an outcome. Two, you have to be able to paint a vivid picture of that outcome. Three, the picture you paint has to be optimistic. *You cannot be a visionary by being pessimistic*. The CEO of General Motors or Ford Motor Company cannot inspire stockholders and retirees by predicting bankruptcy in two years if things don't change. Wall Street analysts can. CEOs cannot.

Here are some sample words you might use:

"When I look down the road, six months from now, here's
what I see."

"When I look out over the horizon, here's what I see."

"Ten months from now, we'll look back at this time as the
moment when we came together."

"One year from now, *we will have the best* people. *We will have
the best* process. *We will have the best* product."

Before we move on to the topic of tailoring your message when
you're answering questions, let's look at an example of a very crisp
message that brings main point, breadth, depth, height, and sight
together.

[Main point] I'm supporting the decision to go forward. And that conclusion is based on three benefits. [Breadth] We'll have a product that
allows our customers to achieve their needs much faster. They'll be
ecstatic at how simple it is to use and maintain. And we are going to see
a quantum leap in revenue in 2007. [Depth] As far as the efficiencies
customers will get, I was talking to ATP's CEO at last week's investor
relations meeting, and he said, "All of us are thrilled at the prospect of a
significantly improved supply chain because of you guys and your product." [Height] While we're so excited about the benefits of the product,
the bigger message here is what this says about the decisions we made
two years ago to invest in a new technology. We have incredible people
in this organization who made this happen. [Sight] When we meet this
time next year, you are going to see bar charts that show us having
gone from third place to first place in our market.

Tailoring Your Message
When the Questions Start

So you have crisply expressed a complex message. Now some of
your listeners will say, "Dale knows how to take a complex message
and lay it out clearly." But it's not over. You have to take questions

too. Your reputation as a person who is "too technical" or "too detailed" results from both your initial message *and* the way you answer everyday questions. I just left a meeting helping a CEO and CFO prepare for an investor "road show" prior to an initial public offering of stock. Both of them mentioned another executive's ability to present their message but his inability to credibly answer potential investors' questions.

Keep Your Answer to the Same Length as the Question

Take a look at this script from the television show *The West Wing*. I encourage you to watch television shows that depict business meetings. I think it's a great idea to watch with the English subtitles so you can see the script (as I did when copying this down). This scene involves senior White House staff members answering questions. Look for two things: (1) the crispness of the answers, and (2) the character's demonstration of depth—but simply done.

> *Question:* Why does the government subsidize television for rich people?
> *Answer:* It's not television for rich people. The public television audience is a fairly accurate reflection of the social and economic makeup of the U.S. Twenty-five percent of the audience has incomes lower than twenty thousand dollars a year.
> *Question:* PBS's claims about most households' being weekly viewers are based on Nielson ratings, which are diaries. The numbers gathered by the automated boxes are much lower. Why?
> *Answer:* People want to claim they are more sophisticated than they are.

The answering character is supposed to be very technically deep on legislation. He advises the president. But the script portrays him as a person who can tailor his message to the audience. Short and sweet.

Here are some randomly chosen questions and answers from the same show.

> *Question:* How long have you been with the public defender's office?
> *Answer:* About two years.

> *Question:* I heard you were at Ross-Lipton. What happened?
> *Answer:* They gave me a corner office.

> *Question:* When does he land?
> *Answer:* Around 9 A.M.

> *Question:* Where will he be?
> *Answer:* I don't know.

> *Question:* Leo, why the seven of us?
> *Answer:* The president wants a lively debate. He wants to hear opposition, but he's not gonna stomach hypocrisy.

Notice that the responses follow a guideline—not a rigid rule, but a guide, one we at CDA have been suggesting for many years: when you think about answering a question, try to keep your answer about the *same length* as the question. This tip, this technique, ensures that you'll come across as having the ability to communicate complex information skillfully. Although most of the questions in the example are pretty easy to answer, one of them is not. "Leo, why the seven of us?" could have led to a very long, protracted explanation. But the character stays true to the rule of "short question, short answer."

Use High School or College Exams as Your Model for Answering Questions Properly

"Will you be ready on time?" *Yes*.

"Will you be ready on time or do you want the deadline extended?" *I'll definitely be ready.*

"What can I do to help you be ready on time?" *Make sure Jim knows that it's a priority.*

"Why weren't you ready on time?" *Jane asked me to fly to London. That required my moving the deadline back.*

Believe it: the four types of questions here represent all the options for the real world of business questions. And there's a handy way to think about them: they are worded very much the same way that college test questions are worded. Test questions fall into four categories:

1. True or false
2. Multiple choice
3. Fill in the blank
4. Essay

Let's look at some examples:

1. The acronym *IMF* stands for the International Monetary Fund. T or F
2. The acronym *IMF* stands for one of the following. Circle one:
   a. International Monetary Fund
   b. International Military Force
   c. Internal Monitoring Field
   d. Investigating and Measuring Facility
3. What does the M in *IMF* stand for? _____
4. Explain why we need the International Monetary Fund.

When you are asked a question, take a moment to think about its form—true or false, multiple choice, fill in the blank, or essay—and tailor your answer accordingly. It will be so much better. It will be truly focused. If your answers are focused, you are on your way to a great reputation as a person who stays at a high level of analysis and doesn't get bogged down in meaningless detail. And that gives your personal credibility a huge jump start.

Take the Thirty-Second Elevator Ride

In Chapter Four, I write about a way of expressing your thoughts that we call *Speak with Logic*. My intent in Chapter Four is to cover all the reasons why someone might be thought of as losing her cool, losing her composure.

But there's a place for Speak with Logic here. All of us are supposed to be able to show our credibility, to sound credible, by expressing a complex issue to a senior executive in a minimum amount of time. Suppose you prepare a thirty-minute presentation for a senior executive. Maybe you have a "deck" (package of presentation papers) or a PowerPoint file with twenty-five slides, or both. Maybe your presentation is toward the end of a day-long meeting. What if the executive says, "Jay, I've got to get out to the airport. Walk down to the limo with me and give me the essence of your presentation." Now we are talking about truly tailoring a message. Here are the steps of this "walk down" or "elevator ride" message:

1. Problem
2. Cause
3. Consequence
4. Solution
5. Action

Here is what you might say:

[Problem] The overall theme of my presentation is a problem we're continuing to see with the call center. We're seeing a lot of turnover. [Cause] I'm claiming that it's due mostly to a lack of proper training, less than competitive hourly pay rates, and a workplace that people say is not safe and secure. [Consequence] We're spending a lot of money, and customers are mad as hell. [Solution] So I am here to suggest we beef up the training program, pay people more, and move to a more secure site. And I have some suggestions on how we could do it.

A credible employee, staff person, or team contributor should be able to simplify a topic that an executive knows has real complexity. That executive will say about you, "Jay knows how valuable his and my time are."

Keep Your Ears Open

Here's another example of the same Speak with Logic template uncovered in an entirely different context.

A few years ago, Jane, the controller of a worldwide oil and gas company, encouraged me to sit in on her staff meetings. Each of eight staff members would present to her in turn. Her questions would often follow this same Speak with Logic pattern. She would look at a spreadsheet and ask, "What the heck is that?"

The presenter might say, [Problem] "We're down in the third quarter."

Jane would, of course, ask, "Why?"

The speaker would offer a reason or say, [Cause] "I don't know."

Then she would say, "What are the short- and long-term effects?" [Consequence] Again, an answer. Finally, Jane might say, [Solution] "How should we report this out? What's the best way to cast this for the CFO?"

At some point, I began a series of seminars with her team. The very first one was a chance for me to say to them, "Look, if you keep your ears open, you'll hear that Jane generally asks questions in this order. Why not construct your presentation around the order?" A team member could say to her, "Jane, I'm going to describe a couple of things we're seeing, then tell you their causes and the short- and long-term consequences, and offer a couple of solutions."

The first time Jane and I ran into each other in the hall, she said, "I don't know specifically what they're learning, but whatever it is, keep doing it. They come across as if they're 'wired in' to the way I think."

Avoid Nested Alternatives, or "Darnit, Advocate a Position"

As I began wrapping up this chapter, I had a conversation with a client that struck me like a thunderbolt. I've been doing this work for a long time and was a little disappointed with myself that this had not come to me sooner.

The client and I were going to have a coaching session about staying "high level." But she gave me a different take on this topic. She said that her boss had been trying to get her to stop laying out so many alternatives. Those alternatives came across to him and his boss as "the weeds." He basically told her, "Advocate a position," but in the end she would chicken out. And as she put it, she chickened out to cover her butt. She (and other team members, for that matter) wanted to make sure senior people had been told about all the ifs, ands, and buts so that nothing could come back to bite her.

Let's look at an example. We don't need a diagram to understand what her boss wanted her to do. He wanted her to say, "We need to develop this product. The regulation as written makes it necessary. Let me go over the regulation for you." Nothing more.

You can see that what the boss was looking for didn't even take wide breadth of analysis. The case was based on one factor alone: "The regulation as written makes the product necessary."

But my client wouldn't quit while she was ahead. Instead, after describing the regulation, she went into the weeds. She began debating, almost with herself. She went on to say, "There are three options in dealing with the regulation. We can go to Legal and see if there's any wiggle room in the way the regulation is written. Or we can lobby to change it. Or we can claim that our current product fits the definition."

Then she actually began to debate the debate. She continued, "There are pros and cons to each of those. Here they are." I'm not going to spell those out, but in diagram form, her presentation looked like Figure 2.4.

Figure 2.4. Getting into the Weeds.

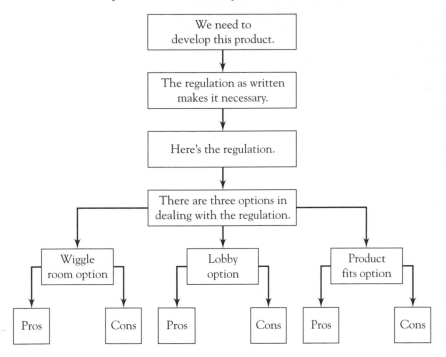

My executive assistant, Marie Lopez, asked me how I would get a client to stop going into the weeds. I said, "I tell her to 'Stop it.'" The simple truth is, all coaching, in the end, comes down to "Do it" or "Stop it."

Subsequently, a former client in a very senior position at the same organization looked at the preceding example and offered this approach:

The problem (or opportunity) is x.

I recommend doing y. The cost/benefit ratio of this is z.

I also considered doing a or b. They fall short of y because their cost/benefit ratios are d and e.

He told me, "I hope this helps. I understand that this sequence is similar to what military officers are trained to do when reporting."

3

SO SMART,
BUT DOESN'T GET IT

After a full day of sitting through a seminar, even one of mine, people need to relax. It's very common for a team to go out together, maybe grab a beer. Not long ago, the supervisor of a team I worked with suggested that very thing. One of the team members declined. He said, in effect, that he felt no obligation to spend time with workmates after work. As we all say, "No biggie." But the supervisor told me that this person had turned down similar invitations a few times. His behavior left the impression that he was not a team player.

If you turn down a chance to socialize with your colleagues, it may mean nothing, but it could come across as a snub. And if it does, you might be considered "So smart, but lacking common sense."

Being imbued with "common sense" is part of the competence factor of the credibility model. In other words, competence includes both intellectual bandwidth and a generally solid instinct for how to handle potentially ambiguous situations.

"So smart, but lacking common sense" pales in comparison to some of the other descriptions I've heard. Here are a few more:

"But doesn't understand our corporate culture"

"But doesn't get it"

"But doesn't have sound judgment"

"But insists on needs assessment"

"But doesn't see the big picture"

So Smart, But Doesn't Understand
Our Corporate Culture

We work with clients positioned all along a wide spectrum of corporate cultures—and that has nothing to do with globalization. I'm speaking about American companies with offices right here in the United States. One way to understand an organization's culture is to look at the degree of consensus required for members to make a decision. You might even hear the words, "We're a consensus culture." The way you see that played out in conference rooms reveals a lot about the company and its employees.

For example, a meeting opens with the leader's laying out the agenda and then saying, "Does that sound all right with everyone?" The leader announces the topic by saying, "We're here to decide how to handle the problems users are having with the new software. Is everyone on board with that?" One participant says, "Can we get agreement first on what these problems are?" Another participant says, "I'm uncomfortable with calling it software. It's a Web-hosted design." The leader says, "How about if we brainstorm the definition of the problem first?"

The newest team member then says, "You all know that I've just joined the company. I came over from IBM, and we didn't approach things this way. I suggest we come up with a solution first and then talk about some of these other issues. We'll save a lot of time." A hush falls over the room. *Hmmm. This guy must think he's too sexy for his shorts. He can't just come in here and change things to suit his likes.*

Is it an art or a science to see, hear, and feel the atmosphere and how you need to adjust? The new member doesn't pick up on the consensus atmosphere in his new organization. He doesn't pick up on the problem-and-solution process his team follows. He doesn't have a feel for how one can successfully bring change to an organization.

On the opposite end of the spectrum you have organizations that actively fight the consensus model. Their meetings sound much more like the back room of the Ba Da Bing club in *The Sopra-*

nos. Leadership Sopranos Style, by Deborrah Himsel (2003), vice president of organizational effectiveness at the Avon Corporation, captures the mood.

Imagine an organization operating with this culture. When the staff meets to talk about problems with software, the leader starts the meeting by saying, "Here's the agenda. Let's get started. Users are complaining about the software. What's new? Just let them live with it?" The new employee says, "I came over from IBM, and we didn't approach things this way. Why don't we go around the room and see if everyone agrees with the premise." The group might think, *Hmmm, he needs to back off the "Kum Ba Ya" crap and get with the program.*

I love one of the many sayings attributed to Anonymous, that a genius looks at the same thing everyone is looking at but sees what no one else sees. Should it take a genius to understand, to look at what is happening in a situation and see what he or she must do to play a part in it? A well-known "expert" on genius, in a manner of speaking, was Frank Sinatra. In the liner notes of one of his albums, he wrote that he had a plan for organizing the numbers he sang in a live concert. "In the first half, I sing the songs the audience has come to love, and I sing them exactly as they have come to love them. I make them comfortable, in other words, with me and with the tone of the evening. Once I have their trust, in the second half, I get a little more experimental. I sing new tunes with new rhythms. The audience is much more receptive that way."

Sinatra is giving us two great tips. First, he is telling us all to keep our ears and eyes open for what the audience wants from us. Second, he's showing us how to bring change: get them to trust you.

So Smart, But Doesn't Get It

I can't think of a more potentially discrediting remark that could be made about a colleague. Sometimes I describe negative perceptions as "pretty benign." Sometimes I describe them as "potentially malignant." "So smart, but doesn't get it" fits the second category.

Typically my clients will hear this comment if (1) they misplay the importance of an issue that others truly believe merits concern or (2) they continually make the same case for every issue.

Not long ago, I was in a coaching session with Bill, a national sales manager in pharmaceuticals. He had a window looking out over a corridor and noticed when one of his subordinates walked by. He said to me, "Hold on a minute, Allen. I need to talk to Larry." He quickly opened the office door and said, "Larry, come in. Have you had a chance to talk with Bob? I'm not happy with the way things are shaping up." Larry said, "Calm down. I've got things under control. There's nothing to worry about. It's not worth it." Larry left the room.

Bill asked me if I could arrange some coaching for Larry. "He doesn't understand that what worries me should worry him. I don't need to be told 'There's nothing to worry about.' There's a lot to be worried about, and he just doesn't get it."

Then there's the issue of continually arguing the same case when an issue comes up. If you look back at Figure 2.3 in Chapter Two, you'll see that one of the eight parts of breadth is the "right thing to do" case. For example, some of my clients think that every decision turns on the right thing to do. It's also referred to as "the ethical case." There's an implied presence of "ethics" when someone says, "I feel like telling the truth is just the 'right thing to do.'"

Recently I sat in on an executive committee meeting in the chemical industry. I had been asked to sit in so I could observe a man whom my firm was going to be coaching. The conversation turned to the issue of when and how to alert the workforce of an impending reduction in force, realignment, redeployment—in other words, that people were to be laid off. One member argued the revenue case (number 1 in Figure 2.3). That is, she said that alerting the workforce too soon would trigger a negative reaction on Wall Street. Someone else seconded that and added that it would also create an immediate response from the labor union.

My client stepped up to the plate and said that it would be "totally unethical and cruel to wait. People must be told immediately. They have families, you know. They have youngsters in school."

At the end of the meeting, the CEO approached me and said, "Your client's attitude on ethics is one you can depend on him to articulate for every argument. He needs to understand the importance of revenue and our long-term survival. He should not be a one-trick pony. In addition to neglecting the concerns some of the rest of us have about revenue, he is implying that we're not thinking about the ethical issues. He's so smart, but just doesn't get it."

I should say at this point that many of my clients think that the boss should simply communicate these attitudes to their subordinates and that the subordinates would then act appropriately and say the right things. But the boss argues that these are the kinds of things that people should not have to be taught. They should just *get it*.

So Smart, But Doesn't Have Sound Judgment

The reason this category stands apart from the others is that *judgment* is defined as the act of coming to an opinion after examining the facts. In the earlier examples, the perception was that my clients just didn't know better, that they weren't making an informed decision. I don't know which is worse:

He weighed the alternatives. It was just a terrible decision.
He didn't think it through. He didn't know better.

Suppose your organization threw a black-tie event to celebrate the huge success of a new product. You were put in charge of the entertainment. You spent a considerable amount of time working with theatrical agents to choose the perfect act. You engaged the act at an exorbitant cost. The comedian was booed off the stage. He used foul language. He insulted various members of the executive committee with inappropriate double entendres.

On Monday morning you are called onto the executive floor to explain how it all happened. It's bad for your boss to find out that you actually knew that the comedian was edgy and unpredictable and still chose to engage him. In fact, you had seen his show before and thought he was pretty good. It's even worse for the boss to find out that you just didn't know better.

A few years ago, our firm was engaged to begin a large project with a very large, old-line law firm. After a few weeks of meetings, the law firm hosted a dinner at an exclusive downtown restaurant. The waiter passed out the menus. Everyone studied them and made individual decisions. When the waiter came to a new associate with the law firm, he said, "I'll have the pâté de fois gras, please." Pâté, as an appetizer, was the most expensive item on the menu. The waiter said, "Do you just want the appetizer instead of dinner?" The fellow replied, "No. I'd like a dinner-size portion."

The others listened with mouths agape—especially those from CDA. This young associate had raised the amount of his firm's dinner tab by nearly the same numbers that he had raised his cholesterol count. It was très embarrassing. It was poor judgment.

Here's another story. I was talking to Rabbi Victor Urecki of B'nai Jacob Synagogue in Charleston, West Virginia. The rabbi is a star of the pulpit. He's known for his speaking and for his "way with people." I had called him to ask about speaking techniques, but he ended up telling me a story that's helpful in a more general way about credibility. He told me about a celebrity who lacked good judgment before a presentation, and it clouded people's perceptions of the presentation itself.

The synagogue invited the celebrity to come to Charleston to speak. This person insisted on a first-class plane ticket. He didn't say, "If it's possible, flying first class would make things so much more comfortable for me, since I'm on the road a lot." The basic message was, "I won't come to Charleston if I don't get a first-class ticket." The congregation "ponied up" the money for the ticket.

The reactions to the presentation itself were clearly colored by the ticket issue. A number of attendees called the speaker condescending. They said, "There was a 'know it all' quality to the message and the delivery style." The rabbi said, "We're not *all* humble and modest, but we tend to be that way, and this speaker was a little too arrogant." This celebrity might have lost an audience for his presentation and might have lost fans over the long term due to a mistake in judgment.

I think consultants show poor judgment in certain billing practices. I've found over the years that my own credibility as a consultant would have been questioned more regarding my travel expenses than my billing rate. We've never charged, for instance, for travel time or first-class airfare. Everyone knows that speakers and consultants build up enough frequent flyer points to go first class whenever they want.

So Smart, But Insists on Needs Assessment

I have encountered hundreds of extremely bright employees, particularly in the training and development side of human resources, who believe in "needs assessment" as if it were a biblical injunction.

What, you might ask, could possibly be wrong with asking people, prior to delivering a training program, what their needs are? If you were hired as a sales trainer from the outside, or if you pursued such a position from within the organization, you would naturally want to please the sales and marketing department. You would want your training to be "tailored to their needs."

I must warn you that your "customers" don't value needs assessment as much as you might think; as a result, they think you are wasting their time. And if they think that you're wasting their time, they will start to question your judgment. They might think, "He's so smart, but he has his priorities confused." They might say, "She's so smart, but she's inflexible about her approach to the training program."

Now here's the potential problem. Too many trainers spend too many weeks assessing needs before actually doing what they were hired to do: prepare the slides and present them. Further, the needs assessment requires a lot of time meeting with the customers, who generally resent having to give it. In addition, needs assessments that involve questionnaires as well as, or in place of, scheduled meetings generate even more resentment. Your customers are likely to think to themselves, "He's wasting time doing pencil work instead of giving us the benefits we wanted when we took him on." A lot of people who actually sell do not have the same confidence in quantitative measures for "sales competencies" as a trainer might. Doing needs assessment in order to develop "competencies" takes even more time without absolute proof of ultimate value.

And there's one more terrible risk that anyone involved in needs assessment must face: the delivered program had better be worth all the time your needs assessment took. All too often, trainers do not deliver. They have boring PowerPoint decks and marginal presentation skills. Their manner is dry. They do not make eye contact. They read bullet points directly off the screen. It can be a nightmare. And after all their needs assessment, a little bit of digging reveals that the deck was a result of "Googling" the words *sales training*.

When companies engage our firm to deliver a training program on credibility, they expect we'll do our "due diligence" to prepare ourselves. They know we might request a few meetings with responsible stakeholders. But just as often, they have heard about a program we've done somewhere else and simply say, "Come in and do for us what you did for them." No needs assessment required. Just be as good as the reputation that precedes you.

Grinders, Minders, and Finders. Consulting firms are a terrific model for all of you engaged in training and development work within your organization. Internally, we've spoken of our employees as grinders, minders, or finders. You may be with a law or accounting firm that thinks of this framework differently, but here is our take on it. Grinders are the employees who do "the work." They are people who know about consulting from the inside out. They conduct interviews, but do not draw relevant conclusions from them. They prepare reports. They are paid to do research, write it up, and get it to relevant decision makers on time. It's technical work and often doesn't get sufficient respect from higher-level contributors. If by the time you are thirty-five you find yourself involved in grinding, you must think about making a change. Needs assessment is grinding.

Minders are people who develop contacts at the client site. They are networkers. They use their interpersonal skills to meet relevant people and get those people engaged in their content area. Those people end up "selling" our services within the organization. Training and development personnel have historically not been skilled minders. If you look at open-ended comments on our Essessnet tool, you will often find statements like, "She needs to get out of her office and network more. She needs to use others in the organization to champion her strategy. She has good ideas but doesn't get them implemented."

Our firm's finders are of immeasurable value. They find us new clients and new engagements. They are our salespeople. Within any organization, a finder reaches out beyond his or her own area, again with great networking skills, to sell people on the benefits of working with his or her department. Finders move from the sales and marketing department over to finance and "sell" their services. If those services are well received, finders have enhanced the greater glory of the training and development function.

We can draw a few conclusions:

Needs assessment without obvious benefit is a waste of time.

Needs assessment is viewed as the work of a grinder.

Minders and finders can be contemptuous of grinders.

Think about a restaurant owner hiring a chef. Should the chef say, "I need a month to assess the needs of your typical diners before I prepare the menu"? Should a chef say to all the customers, "What do you want me to do with your sea bass?" The owner should feel comfortable that a chef has come to the job with a reputation for excellence in the kitchen. The owner should say, "Just cook, and let's see how my customers react. You just do that thing you do, and they'll love you." Now that's not to say that the chef shouldn't make adjustments after getting feedback. She should. That's an appropriate use of time.

If you're hired to do a job, don't overburden your colleagues with assessments. They'll let you know if something needs to change.

So Smart, But Doesn't See the Big Picture

Our firm released our own 360° feedback process two years ago. We call it Essessnet (on the Web at www.essessnet.com). We offer nearly twenty different instruments through which a person can receive feedback. Several of the instruments include a question asking, in essence, "Do I come across as having a broad, strategic view?" We have thousands of individual subscribers. Here are some sample comments about some of those people:

> "Needs more experience in areas other than her own."
>
> "Totally focused on her customers. The company has to be a priority too."
>
> "Not sufficiently aware of what's going on in the industry."
>
> "Unaware of his own talented people."
>
> "Closed off to points of view that run counter to hers."
>
> "Doesn't see that it's his people who make the rubber meet the road."
>
> "Too obsessed with details to stay on top of everything that is going on."

By the way, it is possible to be *too* "big picture." Some people write:

"She's so 'up there' that she doesn't know what it's like down here in the trenches."

"People think of him as a visionary but I think that's just an excuse to avoid daily problem solving."

"She is totally blind to her faults. She thinks she's an angel."

We have developed two techniques based on the notion of a telescope that are intended to change perceptions like those I've listed here.

The Stratescope. We call the first technique *the Stratescope*, as illustrated in Figure 3.1.

The narrowest end of the Stratescope represents your personal view on a topic. You might say, "I think we need to change the way we do things." The next segment represents your team. "Most of the team is on board. We all think it's time for a change." The next

Figure 3.1. The Stratescope.

segment represents the department—marketing, perhaps. You would say, "Marketing as a group has mixed feelings. There is still a lot of selling to do." The next segment up reflects the view of senior management. "I can't speak for everyone on the executive committee or on the board of directors, but I can say that they have a history of being proactive, and I expect they will be in this case too." The last segment represents the industry. You would say, "If you look at industry trends in the last three years, there's a clear move in this direction."

I don't mean to say that you would always express one viewpoint after the other in every opportunity you have to speak up. I do want you to express these as independent thoughts over the course of the decision-making process.

A Credible Leader's Three Visions. Another technique we encourage is called *A Credible Leader's Three Visions.* It also uses the telescope as a metaphor for your ability to be a "visionary." There are three perspectives, three visions if you will, that you must demonstrate on a regular basis. I call them *in-sight, near-sight, and far-sight.* (See Figure 3.2.)

In-sight represents your ability to see into yourself and talk about what you see. People who come across as blind to their own faults are, interestingly enough, perceived as not being big-picture people. Near-sight represents your ability to see the people who work with you and for you—and talk about them. A person who seems blind to the talents of colleagues cannot have 20-20 vision. Far-sight represents your ability, the more traditional visionary's ability, to see over the horizon and, once again, talk about it.

Figure 3.2. Three Visions.

In-Sight	Near-Sight	Far-Sight
"I know I can be impatient sometimes. I know I don't always listen."	"I know how much all of you mean to this effort. I never forget who really stirs the drinks."	"When I look out there at what's just around the bend, I see a consumer who can't wait to get his hands on this."

But people need you to do more than talk about your vision. In addition to expressing your three visions verbally, you have to "do things," and you have to aggressively react in a way that drives home your visionary talent. Figure 3.3 illustrates this idea with examples, and I'll discuss each of the visions in turn in the next sections.

You Show In-Sight Through What You Do.   Whatever we might *say* about ourselves, what we *do* also reveals who we are. The credible person reveals information as soon as possible.

One of my patrons (I use *patron* to describe someone who "brings us in" to his or her organization), shared something that makes so much

Figure 3.3. Leadership Vision.

In-Sight (Who I am)

What I Say	What I Do	How I React
"I've tended toward holding my cards close to the vest. My dad was the same way."	I communicate what I know as soon as I can.	I attend with total focus to your suggestions for me to be better.

Near-Sight (What you mean to me)

What I Say	What I Do	How I React
"All of you make this work. Our *asset is you.* I know the level of talent we have here."	I promote from within.	I demonstrate that I've chosen you.

Far-Sight (What I dream)

What I Say	What I Do	How I React
"We're creating the model for the twenty-first century."	I support the purchase or development of world-class technology.	I attend with total focus to your ideas for achieving our vision.

sense. She said that doing well during times of change takes a lot of effort on the part of both the organization and the employee.

She said, "The most valuable employee, the one we most want to hold on to for dear life, has a very high tolerance for ambiguity. He or she does not expect or demand constant answers to questions in order to lower the stress level. That said, our leaders need to demonstrate a desire to lower stress levels by getting information to people as soon as we can. That act of talking about things as soon as we can is nearly as important as the message itself."

You Show In-Sight Through How You React. Whenever possible, as you get involved in conversations with others, it should be obvious to them that you are fully open and engaged as they give you suggestions. Remember, we are talking about showing your desire to learn about yourself.

I was working in China some time ago. One of my clients used our 360° feedback tool. One of the questions was, "Do I accept or at least acknowledge your insights about me, or do I get defensive?" Scoring was based on a scale of 1 ("Never") to 5 ("Always"). My client made a big point of how he prided himself on being good at taking in constructive criticism. Of course, a lot of people have a pretty high bar for what they consider *constructive* criticism. My client's boss scored this question 2, "Rarely." What does my client do? He goes to his boss and says, "How can you say that about me? You know that's not true. I can handle constructive criticism. Period. End of story."

Don't do things like that.

You Show Near-Sight Through What You Do. Near-sight is shorthand for your ability to "see," to "have a vision of" the people around you. In addition to telling them how important they are, you have to show it. In Figure 3.3 I give the example of promoting from within whenever you can or whenever you have input on the decision. But there are many other ways to do it. Showing people that you want to get them exposed to senior management by including them in meetings builds their confidence in your goodwill toward them.

There are entire books focusing on management skills, including your attitude toward delegating, so I won't repeat all that here. I will repeat the adage: "Don't worry so much about whether they are listening to you. Remember they are always watching you."

You Show Near-Sight Through How You React. I speak in more detail in Chapter Seven as to my belief that flattery is at the heart of everyone's reactions to you. A person will find it extremely flattering to know that you have set everything else aside so you can pay total attention to him or her. It makes the person feel "chosen." If you want to obviously show you have near-sight through how you react—and you should want to—people have to see it in your manner. Put everything down. No BlackBerry. No TV.

You Show Far-Sight Through What You Do. Whenever you invest in the organization or suggest investments in capital improvements or talent, you've communicated your far-sight. When you promote training and development in such areas as change management, you have shown far-sight.

You Show Far-Sight Through How You React. As coworkers make suggestions about getting ready for the future, you have to show your openness. I have suffered personally as a result of trivializing the input of team members who had a better vision for the future than I did. I am so fortunate that these kinds of experiences happened early in my career and gave me a chance to improve.

In 1996, we hired a young man for our consulting staff. He came to us as enthusiastically as anyone ever has. He immediately pushed for our firm to get a website and to begin using it as a way to market our services. I didn't merely resist the idea—according to the young man in question, I acted as though he were a young pup. He bided his time, built more and more credibility, and finally succeeded in pushing us, meaning me, into the twenty-first century. Can you see how easy it would be for someone to say, "Allen doesn't have vision," simply as a result of my reactions to someone else's vision? (Of course, I'm the guy who told his dad that the Beatles would fade after "I Want to Hold Your Hand" and that Southwest Airlines was not going to attract a lot of customers.)

4

SO SMART, BUT SOUNDS LIKE SHE LACKS EXECUTIVE PRESENCE

In 1981, I received a call from a human resources manager at a Philadelphia-based oil and gas company. He told me that an executive from Philadelphia was currently on loan to the corporate planning group in Los Angeles. The manager struggled through a description of this fellow's credibility issues, but was in essence trying to tell me that Joe didn't have "executive presence."

Some of Joe's problems centered on not looking the part, and some focused on not sounding the part.

He didn't look the part, the manager said, because his hair wasn't properly coiffed. His hair had a more old-fashioned Bryl Cream look (do any of you remember Bryl Cream?) that made it too wet and pasted down. The Los Angeles group, by that time, thought the dry look was more appropriate for an executive. In addition, Joe had "the Philadelphia sound" as an accent, meaning that he substituted "z" for "s" and said things like "gazoline" instead of "gasoline." (When Joe and I first met, he even described his hair as "greazy.")

Joe had a wonderfully good-humored reaction to the feedback and was a proper "Los Angeles Country Club set" executive within a few weeks. He looked like one and sounded like one.

This story reminds us that (1) the people who are judging you think that you should be like them, and (2) every quality on which you are judged has both a look and a sound to it. When people talk about "executive presence," they are talking about the credibility factor we call *composure*.

Composure is a measure of how well you have things under control. When you have things under control, the people who are looking to you for that quality of control experience significantly less stress. That is precisely why you have to show control: it reduces the stress of the people around you. Did Joe's accent and hairstyle increase the stress of the management team in Los Angeles? It probably did. They must have had some stress wondering how Joe would look to some of their external customers or to the board. Here's another way to put it: anyone who feels a lot of doubt or confusion about how you will perform will experience some level of stress. When you reduce that "stress," they are very, very pleased.

Among other things, *to compose* means "to put in proper form." There are several variables that contribute to proper form, and because this chapter is devoted to *sounding* composed and organized, we're going to look more closely at the following:

- The way you organize your message
- The way you array your sentences
- The way you choose your words

I am going to begin by covering three high-impact ways to organize a credible message. The first is called *Get to the Point*. We call the second *Speak with Logic*, and the third is called *Bottom Line Last*.

Get to the Point

In many ways, our firm owes our initial success to the entire notion of getting to the point. If ever the phrase *first and foremost* has truth, the ranking of Get to the Point applies. We have had more requests for seminars and coaching on this issue than on any other single issue in the credibility universe. Apparently, not enough employees are "getting to the point" in their speaking or writing.

Do you remember the definitions of inductive and deductive reasoning? People get them as confused as the difference between *effect* and *affect*. Inductive reasoning is the process of deriving a general principle from particular facts. Deductive reasoning moves from the general to the specific. Many of us were taught, in one class or another, the deductive syllogism "All men are mortal. Steve is a man. Steve is mortal." Although there are exceptions, most listeners prefer hearing messages that start with the general conclusion, or what they often call the "bottom line," and end with facts to back it up. In a business setting, the syllogism would be something along these lines: "All start-ups are a gamble. This is a start-up. This is a gamble."

I learned about getting to the point as part of a debate class. Stephen Toulmin (1958), a rhetorical theorist and now professor emeritus at USC, developed the Toulmin Model of Argument for debaters. He wrote, "if we are to set our arguments out with complete logical candor, and understand properly the nature of 'the logical process,' we shall need to employ a pattern of argument no less sophisticated than is required in the law" (p. 89).

Toulmin wrote that a *claim* is a conclusion "whose merits we seek to establish." A *warrant* is additional information. *Data* are the facts "we appeal to as a foundation for the claim." Figure 4.1 illustrates the model; Figure 4.2 is an example of using the model to

Figure 4.1. Toulmin's Model of Argument.

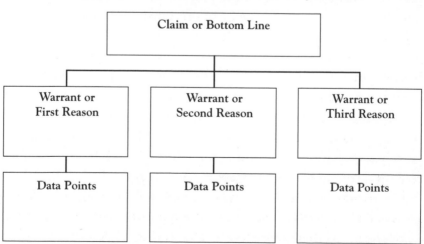

Figure 4.2. Example of Toulmin's Model in Action.

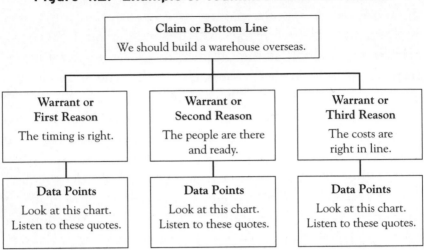

express a point of view. (You might notice that Toulmin's model corresponds to the main point, breadth, and depth components of projecting your intellect that I discuss in Chapter Two.)

Many professionals with a scientific or engineering background will organize their thoughts inductively. That is, they will put the facts first and the conclusion last. They often say to me, "Allen, it's the way we were trained." In spite of the fact that their listeners very often flip to the last slides of a presentation deck to look for the conclusion, these people persist in presenting this way. Even professionals with an MBA in finance will argue that they have to build a case for the conclusion or the conclusion will be rejected before they can support it. The fact is, however, almost all listeners want the conclusion first. They *demand* the conclusion first.

In a recent client engagement, the person sponsoring the seminar told me that he did not care if any of the presenters learned gestures or posture or eye contact. He just wanted them to be able to draw a conclusion and support it. More specifically he said, "The failure to draw a conclusion and to state it reflects someone's desire to avoid taking a risk." I told the participants that it's one thing for someone to say that failure to get to the point comes across as tiresome. But it's an entirely different matter if your boss says, "He or she is not a risk taker."

One important place to get to the point is in your opening to a briefing or presentation. You are also expected to get to the point when you answer questions. And every e-mail reader wants you to get to the point when you write. In the case of the briefing, when someone at the meeting says, "Cindy, you're up. What have you got for us today?" you have to start with words like, "I'm here to make the case that we need to get out of this arrangement as soon as possible. There are three reasons, and I'm going to take them one at a time. First, we're losing money. Second, we're draining resources, and third, we have other priorities. Let's start with the money piece. Take a look at these numbers."

So Smart and Has "Good Weed"

Only a few short weeks ago, I had a terrific conversation with a client that led to a new consulting framework: good weed. Using *weeds* to describe useless detail is pretty common. But using *weed* as a pun for useful detail made us both smile. The client told me that her boss often reminded her to stay out of the weeds. "Too detailed" can mean a lot of things, and almost all of them are bad—bad weed so to speak. Here are just a few examples:

Qualifying

Repeating yourself

Rambling

Going over data without characterizing their meaning

I told her to tell her boss that, although he was right about some of her behavior, all her weed wasn't bad weed. She had some good weed—some excellent detail. Any data point in the form of a number that proves the validity of a reason, any data point in the form of an anecdote that proves the validity of a reason, is very excellent weed. It's necessary, you might say, for enhancing the communicative experience.

It's About the Time, It's Not About the Watch

I suggested techniques for answering questions in Chapter Two. Here's a little more advice about that in the context of organizing your thoughts on the fly. You have to get to the point answering questions. People commonly complain that when they ask someone for the time, they get an explanation about how a watch is made.

When someone at the meeting says, "What's your confidence level in our ability to transition out of there quickly?" you have to start your answer with words like, "It's high." You cannot start your answer with, "It depends on a number of factors," and then take listeners through all those factors without directly answering the question. You *can* say, "It's high, but it depends on a number of factors."

If you were writing about this topic in an e-mail, your subject line should be, "Recommendation." The opening line of the e-mail would be, "I'm writing to make the case that we get out of the *x* arrangement as soon as possible."

Speak with Logic

In the section "Take the Thirty-Second Elevator Ride" in Chapter Two, I talked about a form of Speak with Logic, and I want to flesh it out here. Figure 4.3 lays out the process. There are a few things I want you to notice about it going in. First, it puts a lot of emphasis on *the solution*. We encourage you to have most of your content there. Second, you are forced to cover both the downsides and upsides of your solution. It's not an accident that we encourage you to start with the downsides and end with the upsides. Speakers who are thought of as composed get the "bad news" out of the way quickly and put most of their emphasis on the good news. Finally, you must end with an *action step* that is much more specific and time oriented than the solution. After you look at Figure 4.3, read through the example that follows.

Figure 4.3. Speak with Logic.

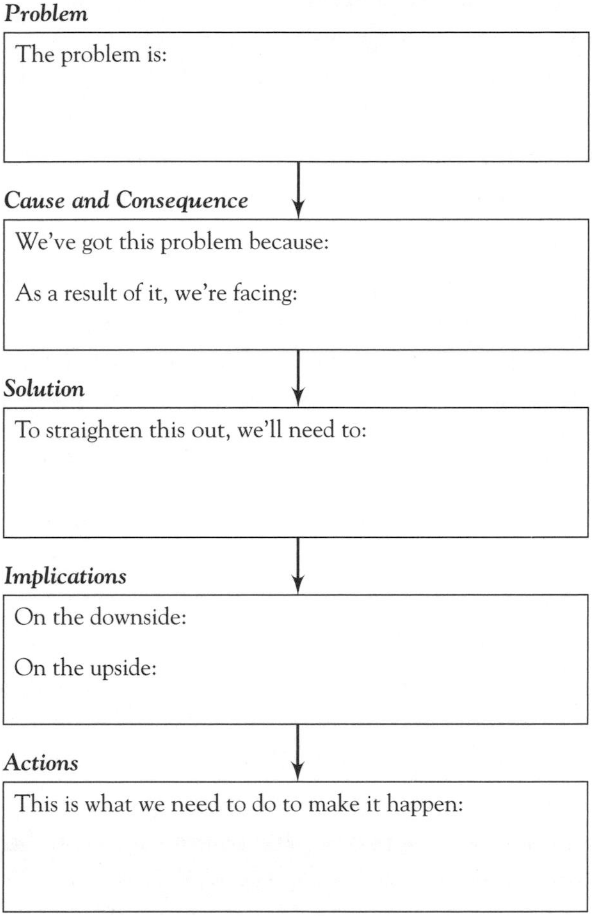

Problem

> The problem is:

Cause and Consequence

> We've got this problem because:
>
> As a result of it, we're facing:

Solution

> To straighten this out, we'll need to:

Implications

> On the downside:
>
> On the upside:

Actions

> This is what we need to do to make it happen:

Ask yourself if you can imagine using this kind of flow. By the way, we call it Speak with Logic because focus groups feel that people who speak this way seem not only composed but also logical.

Imagine yourself speaking in front of a group of people who are looking to you for a solution to a very nagging problem. Following the step-by-step process of Speak with Logic, you might say,

As you know, we've been struggling with a nasty supply chain problem for nearly two years. Customers are complaining that their warehouses are overflowing with inventory that they cannot move. They are worried about time-stamped goods that have a limited shelf life. [You probably have a few PowerPoint slides that depict the problem.]

There are a few things that are causing our problem. We're in an area of the world that is slow to change. Our technology is not as effective here as it is in other parts of the world. There are a myriad of cultural nuances that we need to get on top of. [PowerPoint slides]

In any event, the consequences are obvious. We're bleeding capital, and we're bordering on losing the trust and confidence of a number of very big players in our business. [PowerPoint slides again]

We're proposing today that we move up the timeline for installing the Supply Chain Megazord Technology (SCMT). Over the next half hour, I'm going to show you exactly how we plan to do that. [more PowerPoint slides]

Are there going to be some problems in the early going? Yes. No doubt there will be. We'll experience some of the growing pains that come with any new technology, including money spent on technical training and a call center for customer service.

But there is so much positive to look forward to. Within six months, we're going to see customers with properly stocked warehouses. We'll hear about end users with smiles on their faces as a result of up-to-the-minute time dating.

With your approval, we're going to pull the trigger on the initiative on August first.

I'll be happy to take your questions.

I wrote this sample imagining you making a presentation.

I want to stress, however, that it's appropriate for an informal discussion, an e-mail, or, with a little tailoring, a voice mail.

Bottom Line Last

Figure 4.4 is a graphical representation of *Bottom Line Last*, a very effective technique for dealing with another very nerve-wracking scenario, one in which you *must* show composure in order to show

Figure 4.4. Bottom Line Last.

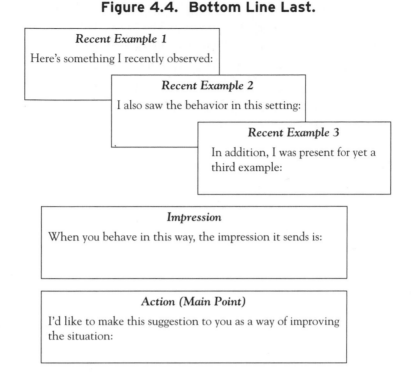

Recent Example 1

Here's something I recently observed:

Recent Example 2

I also saw the behavior in this setting:

Recent Example 3

In addition, I was present for yet a third example:

Impression

When you behave in this way, the impression it sends is:

Action (Main Point)

I'd like to make this suggestion to you as a way of improving the situation:

maximum credibility. Bottom Line Last is used for giving performance feedback—generally speaking, critical (negative) feedback. If your feedback were entirely positive, you would no doubt feel and act more composed when giving it.

Imagine a performance discussion. We hope you are the kind of person who tries to give feedback on an ongoing basis whether it is negative or positive, but maybe you tend to avoid negative issues until a direct report's end-of-year review. In any case (and again, I certainly encourage you to give feedback promptly), using Bottom Line Last is the most composed way to lay out your thoughts. The following is an example of the approach. Notice as you go along that the direct report gets a little defensive and notice how you handle it.

You: Jeremy, may I come in for a minute?
Direct Report: Sure. Sit down.

You: I wanted to take some time, if this works for you, to give you some impressions I've been getting.

Direct Report: Absolutely. What's on your mind?

You: This morning, I noticed you raising your voice to my administrative coordinator for not letting you in to see me. You were pretty vocal about it, and I couldn't help but hear it.

Direct Report: I've always felt that she treated me in a condescending way.

You: I want to talk to her about it, but right now, I'd really like to talk to you.

Direct Report: OK. I'm sorry. Go on.

You: I also noticed the way you treated Gary in yesterday's meeting. He might have been out of line, but I didn't think it was appropriate for you to criticize his grammar in front of everyone.

Direct Report: Yes. I felt bad about that.

You: I'm glad to hear you say that. Finally, and I should've mentioned this after it happened: when the team agreed to meet for breakfast last month, I couldn't help but notice you saying that breakfast was inconvenient for you.

When you do this kind of thing, the impression it makes is that you are making enemies of people who want very much to work with you as an equal. I don't think, and they don't think, that you intend to be so unfriendly, but that's how it comes across.

Direct Report: I think you and they are being a little unfair. There were a lot of extenuating circumstances.

You: While all that may be true, I want so much for you to know the impression it's making.

Direct Report: Yep. I don't want to get off on the wrong foot.

You: That's exactly what I want to avoid. So I'd encourage you to go out of your way to cooperate and to show that you realize we're an interdependent team. We need each other if we're going to be all we can be.

Direct Report: I hear you.

Tailor-Made Templates

In the same conversation about good weed, my client told me that her boss expressed, unintentionally, a preference for information presented in a unique order. I've had a few clients tell me something akin to this—about an executive with a preference for a particular order of information. (I also address this subject in Chapter Two.) Of course I told her to "render unto Caesar" what he wants if it's not asking too much.

Here's what she said:

"He first wants to know what the issue is. Then he wants to know why he should care about it. Then he wants to know if there might be some impact to the company, and finally he wants to know what he needs to do, if anything, to address it." So we invented a framework called I-WIN. All consultants and consulting firms need very clever frameworks, and frameworks that make a good acronym are terrific.

I—the Issue

W—Why he should care

I—the Impact to the organization

N—what he Needs to do to address the issue

She might say, "I've got an issue with our cardboard supplier. They're asking us to accept a three percent cost increase. You need to know about it because you'll be asked about it, and I want you to be prepared. I don't think it will have a material effect on the company's bottom line. You might want to call Delia Jeffords yourself if you think you can change their mind."

An executive with the same organization brought a unique framework with him when he arrived. It carries the acronym OPPC—a good framework that in this case doesn't spell a word:

O—Opportunity

P—Promise

P—Proof

C—Conviction

A presenter might say to this executive, "We have an opportunity in Kazakhstan. It promises to deliver a significant contribution to our revenue stream. Let me show you the numbers. And if we do, and I believe we should, let's go all out or not do it at all."

While I'm on this example, there's one word and a message it sends that I want to mention. The Promise line included the word "significant" as the modifier, and I chose that word on purpose. I might have used "tremendous" or "phenomenal" or "unbelievable" or "incredible," but I did not. Many, many senior executives are turned off by hyperbole when it's used to describe results. I implore you to stay within certain boundaries when doing this so as to reduce your risk of being called naïve. The phrase "underpromise and overdeliver" is highly appropriate in this context. You might describe your team as phenomenal. You might call your team's effort this year incredible. You could refer to a salesperson as having done a tremendous job under the circumstances. But avoid such terms when you're talking about results or predictions of results. People yes. Results no.

So Smart, But Not Articulate: Improving Your Syntax

We at CDA have come to believe that the single greatest differentiating factor in the area of composure is proper syntax. Check your dictionary. *Syntax* is defined as "an orderly or systematic arrangement of words as elements in a sentence" (McKechnie, 1983). Most speakers neglect syntax. When you hear a person who pays attention to it, you will no doubt think to yourself, "She is incredibly articulate . . . incredibly composed . . . a person with 'executive demeanor.'"

Tim Wendel, in an April 27, 2006, piece in *USA Today*, reminded us all that "as in business, entertainment and politics, the best players and *leaders* [emphasis mine] often come from the most unlikely places. Time after time, the fastest, the smartest or the best-connected player doesn't become the next superstar." One of his examples was Winston Churchill. "Growing up, Winston Churchill struggled to master any language, even English. But being held back in school had its benefits. 'I got into my bones the essential structure of the ordinary British sentence—which is a noble thing,' he later said. Noble enough to rally a country at wartime." When I hear a clear thought from a client, I always say, "Well said. Beautifully said."

I'm going to display samples of speeches by three presidents who have been described as being gifted communicators: Franklin Roosevelt, Ronald Reagan, and Bill Clinton. Please put your political affiliations down for a moment. Don't let those attitudes get in the way of objectivity about communication skill. All of these examples are models of proper syntax. *Look first at simple sentences and simple words. Check out the underscored portions.*

In the first example, Roosevelt addresses the nation in celebration of Jackson Day, in Fort Lauderdale, Florida, April 1, 1941.

> I try to get away a couple of times a year on these short trips on salt water. In Washington, as you know, the working day of the Presidency averages about fifteen hours. Even when I go to Hyde Park or to Warm Springs, the White House office, the callers and telephone all follow me. But at sea the radio messages and the occasional pouch of mail reduce official work to not more than two or three hours a day.
>
> That is why, in the comparative quiet of this week, I have become more than ever clear that the time calls for courage and more courage . . . action and more action.
>
> In our own day the threat to our Union and to our democracy is not a sectional one. It comes from a great part of the world that surrounds us. And which draws more tightly around us day by day.

The second example is from President Ronald Reagan's farewell address, given at the White House, Washington, D.C., January 11, 1989.

> One of the things about the presidency is that you're always somewhat apart. You spend a lot of time going by too fast in a car someone else is driving, and seeing the people through tinted glass—the parents

holding up a child, and the wave you saw too late and couldn't return. And so many times I wanted to stop and reach out from behind the glass, and connect. Well, maybe I can do a little of that tonight.

People ask how I feel about leaving. And, the fact is, "parting is such sweet sorrow." The sweet part is California, the ranch and freedom. The sorrow—the good-byes, of course, and leaving this beautiful place. You know, down the hall and up the stairs from this office is the part of the White House where the president and his family live. There are a few favorite windows I have up there that I like to stand and look out of early in the morning. The view is over the grounds here to the Washington Monument, and then the Mall and the Jefferson Memorial. But on mornings when the humidity is low, you can see past the Jefferson to the river, the Potomac, and the Virginia shore. Someone said that's the view Lincoln had when he saw the smoke rising from the Battle of Bull Run. Well, I see more prosaic things: the grass on the banks, the morning traffic as people make their way to work, now and then a sailboat on the river.

The third example is from President Bill Clinton's farewell address, given at the White House, Washington, D.C., January 18, 2001.

Then, in turmoil and triumph, that promise exploded onto the world stage to make this the American Century.

And what a century it has been. America became the world's mightiest industrial power; saved the world from tyranny in two world wars and a long cold war; and time and again, reached out across the globe to millions who, like us, longed for the blessings of liberty.

Along the way, Americans produced a great middle class and security in an old age. We built unrivaled centers of learning and opened public schools to all. We split the atom and explored the heavens. We invented the computer and the microchip; and deepened the wellspring of justice by making a revolution in civil rights for

African Americans and all minorities, and extending the circle of citizenship, opportunity and dignity to women.

In comparison, here's a slice of content from a recent presentation sent to me by a client.

And my assertion is that if in long lead custom, custom versus a commodity market if you're not managing that back into your . . . in unison then the cost of the errors is exponentially worse and you're not always gonna find it and you're going to do it later and, you know what, it's unacceptable.

The audience evaluations described this person as so smart, but unclear, nervous, and unprepared. He could have said the same thing this way:

In a long lead custom market, you must manage that back in unison. If you don't, the cost of errors is exponentially worse. You won't always find it. You'll do it later. You know what? It's unacceptable.

So Smart, But Has Brain Drool

A client pointed out a behavior he called "brain drool," or the drooling of odd words and sounds at the end of a sentence that have no added value. Suppose you intended to say, "The auditors are jacking us around. It happens all the time. I've gotten used to it, but I'm going to really express myself this time." In that version, the speaker sounds confident. Can you hear that as you read it to yourself?

Here's the same thought with brain drool: "The auditors are jacking us around and uhhh, uhhh, well, ummm and it happens all the time and . . . and uhhh, ummm, I've gotten used to it, used to it, but ummm . . ." You get the idea. It's a bit irritating to have to read all the umms and uhhhs, but they evoke the feeling of drool all too effectively. It would be such a shame to take the power of the intended message and dilute it so dramatically.

Improving Your Word Choice

In our research, listeners continually voice a preference for one-syllable English. Or I could say, listeners like the sound of one-syllable words. Here is a section of another client's presentation. He's a professor at Harvard. Does he sound less educated because he uses short words? His audience doesn't think so.

> A few comments before I start. Stop me at any point and we'll debate whatever you'd like to discuss.
>
> My topic today is a book I wrote. It's been a year and half since the book came out. Several of the companies are profiled in the book. Most of them I took out of this talk. I didn't want to talk about anybody who is in the room. In fact, one thing again . . . either I was lucky or something . . . but the only company in my book that I profiled that is no longer a self-sustaining company happens to be Dave's.
>
> I wrote this during the boom. Every company I wrote about is still alive or doing well. I think everybody is still on a reasonable path. That's the good news.

Many seminar audiences rebel at the thought of simple English. Many of them think that big words equal big ideas. Many of them think that big words equal big brains. Although it's true that some unique English words can appear to make the speaker "well versed," most do not. In Reagan's speech earlier, he used the word *prosaic*. It works. But generally, a more complex, three-syllable version of a perfectly clear, one-syllable English word only serves to make a speaker's message harder to follow. What follows is an example of what the first paragraph of Reagan's speech might have looked like if a writer preferring "bigger" words had drafted it:

One of the particulars concerning the presidency is that you're consistently somewhat divergent. You spend considerable amounts of
time traveling too quickly in an automobile someone else is driving,
and seeing the people through tinted glass—the parents holding up
a child, and the wave you saw too late and couldn't return. And so
many times I wanted to stop and reach out from behind the glass, and
connect. Well, perhaps I can accomplish a modicum of that tonight.

Reagan would not have been called the Great Communicator.
And while I'm on President Reagan, a popular pundit, Joe Klein,
was recently asked on Chris Matthew's television show why Repub-
licans are thought to be clearer communicators than Democrats. He
said, "Because they use short sentences or even fragments of sentences." Klein is a columnist for *Time* magazine. His sixth book is
*Politics Lost: How American Democracy Was Trivialized by People Who
Think You're Stupid.*

Using Pauses as Accents

I remember telling my parents that I'd read some interesting research
about vocalized pauses. I was still an undergraduate. My dad was not
too excited about the topic and was probably worried about my fas-
cination with it, but I couldn't help myself.

For an armoire to stand out, it has to be placed against a blank
wall. For a piece of jewelry to stand out, it has to be placed against
the blank backdrop of skin. For a photographer's subject to stand
out, it has to be placed against the horizon or a simple background.
And for a sentence to stand out, it has to be placed against a pause.
When sentences are so placed, the speaker sounds composed and
prepared. Every sentence stands out as a useful part of the whole
story. Here's a slice of presentation with no pauses, followed by an
edited version of the speaker's notes.

They are going all restricted stock they've eliminated options it's a
questionable choice but that's what they're doing they are however

for the top six hundred officers attaching performance contingents to that restricted stock which is something they wouldn't have done in the current accounting environment but it's something they can do without whole new extra charges in a fair value accounting world so it's one of the reasons they would adopt fair value as attractive to them.

They are going all restricted stock.

They've eliminated options.

It's a questionable choice, but that's what they're doing.

They are, however, for the top six hundred officers, attaching contingents. That is something they wouldn't have done in the current accounting environment.

But it's something they can do without whole new extra charges in a fair value accounting world.

It's one of the reasons they would adopt fair value as attractive to them.

Can you get a feel for how this presentation would have sounded to you had you been there?

A close relative of failing to pause is the terrible habit of connecting sentences with "and," "but," or "so." And to add insult to injury, these words are often accompanied by brain drool, our infamous "uhhh." The same script would sound like this:

They are going all restricted stock and uhhh they've eliminated options and uhhh it's a questionable choice but uhhh that's what they're doing. They are however uhhh for the top six hundred officers attaching performance contingents to that restricted stock which uhhh is something they wouldn't have done in the current accounting environment but uhhh it's something they can do without whole new extra charges in a fair value accounting world so uhhh it's one of the reasons they would adopt fair value as attractive to them.

If ever there were a case of "So smart, but he sounds unprepared," it would have to be this kind of thing.

Vowels and Consonants

If you consciously choose whether to stress the vowels or the consonants in a spoken phrase, you can control the level of certainty you want to express. Say the next sentence to yourself. "I think we need to revise our position when it comes to reimbursement policy." Now I'm going to write the sentence the way it sounds, capitalizing the consonants for emphasis. Say it out loud.

I ThinK We NeeD To ReViZe our PoSition Wen iT KumZ To ReimBurSemenT.

Now I'm going to spell it out with the emphasis on the vowels. Say it out loud.

I think wEE nEEEd to rEEvIIze our pUHHsition when IIIt cUHHHms to rEEEimbUUUrsment.

The first version will sound significantly more decisive and more confident.

I became fascinated with this technique after hearing a Broadway and movie star, Hugh Jackman, explaining how he approaches the song "My Boy Bill" in the show *Carousel*. He explains that Steven Sondheim, who wrote the song, intended for the character to emphasize each consonant so that he would sound certain about the future of his boy. The full lyric is, "My boy Bill will be as strong and as tough as a tree." Say the line to yourself emphasizing the *B* in "boy" and "Bill," the *S* in "strong," and the *T* in "tough" and "tree." Can you hear how the character would sound so sure of himself? Now say it with the emphasis on the vowels. Can you hear how it sounds musical, but lacks the tone of certainty? (Technical lessons out of the art of singing are very difficult to find. Singers do not like making technical suggestions. They simply say, "You have to be in the moment and feel the music." That's not bad advice for a communicator, but communication skills imply the use of techniques, which is why I wrote *So Smart But . . .*)

Takeoffs and Landings

There have been so many times when I've heard clients who seem to have trouble getting a sentence off the ground. Let's suppose you intended to start a speech with the words, "There was a young man walking home from a Little League game." Think of it. Someone introduces you, and you walk to the lectern. The plane leaves the gate. You say, "Good afternoon." Fine. The plane begins to taxi to the runway. Then you say, "It's a pleasure to be here." Again, fine. The plane begins to roll. Then you say, "I always look forward to the opportunity to talk about my favorite subject." All right. The plane is gaining speed. Then you clear your throat. "Ahem. Excuse me." The plane is still rolling. Then you say, "I'd like to, uhhh, start this presentation with a story." Not so good. The plane hits some bumps on the runway. Then you say, "I hope you like the story because, uhhh, it has so much to say about seeing the big, uhhh, picture, and, uhhh, that's a big part of my mission, uhhh today." Very bad. The tower is issuing a warning: Take off. Take the hell off! So you do. You get the sentence off the ground.

The next sentence was intended to be, "The boy was draping his bat on his right shoulder, and he had a ball in his left hand." You begin your descent toward a crisp, sharp, perfect landing of this sentence. "The boy was draping his bat . . ." Uh-oh, the plane starts to hit some turbulence. "The boy was kind of draping his bat on his, his uhhh right uhhh shoulder and had, he had a ball, his ball . . . let's see, 'right shoulder' . . . yeah right . . . in his left hand . . . and then uhhh." The plane has a very rough and bumpy landing. The passengers are wondering, *Who the heck is flying this thing?*

To sound composed and polished, you have to keep your sentences reasonably short, roll them down the runway, have an uplifting takeoff, and then land them with confidence.

Primacy-Recency:
Start Negative But End Positive

Over the years there have always been times when I've fallen in love with communication studies all over again. It still happens. It happens because I'll read about research that is so darn interesting that I can't wait to try it with a client. I immediately get the feeling that a very small behavioral step will have a huge positive outcome.

One of the most exciting distinctions I've ever read about was an area of study called primacy-recency. Primacy-recency describes the phenomenon of what comes first and what comes last. In the study of communication, of course, it's about the first part of a message and the last part—the beginning and the end. It's important to include a discussion of this notion in *So Smart, But . . .* because so many of our clients are described as pessimistic and negative.

Leave Listeners with a Good Taste

Pessimism contributes a lot to colleagues' perceptions of this composure piece of the overall credibility puzzle. When you are viewed as upbeat and positive, you will be described as having more composure. Look at the following pairs of examples. Which is the better way for the speaker to express herself?

A. "You're doing a great job, but you still have some things to work on." (starts positive [P], ends negative [N]) The listener feels "you're doing a great job" was glossed over.

B. "You still have some things to work on, but you're doing a great job." (starts N, ends P) The listener feels "you're doing a great job" is the intended message.

A. "We've come a long way this year, but it's going to be a struggle to get where we need to go." (starts P, ends N) The listener feels "we've come a long way" was just a bone.

B. "It's going to be a struggle to get where we need to go, but we've come a long way this year." (starts N, ends P) The listener feels "we've come a long way" was the intended message.

A. "I know the figures are correct, but I don't know exactly how we did the calculations." (starts P, ends N) The listener feels the speaker is calling attention to the poor process and not the result.

B. "I don't know exactly how we did the calculations, but I do know the figures are correct." (starts N, ends P) The listener feels the speaker is happy that the figures are right.

A. "I love you, but I don't like your grades." (starts P, ends N) The child feels, "yeah, right," on the "love you" part.

B. "I don't like your grades, but I love you." (starts N, ends P) The child feels, "Well, OK. I'm loved."

Figures of Speech

My favorite communication skills are the classic figures of speech. Most of us learned them (if we were taught them at all) in high school English class, and that was too early in our lives for them to make an impression. I have had a devil of a time persuading clients to use them.

The figures of speech are not a simple lesson. They're for people who want something a little more advanced. At the firm, we've sometimes smiled about requests for seminars that are "not just the basics, but something more advanced." If there is such a notion as basic and advanced, then the figures of speech fall into the second category. They are a little more difficult to master, but their impact is profound. Maybe the reason behind everyone's hesitation about latching on to them is their Greek names. Everyone knows metaphor and simile, but few know epizeuxis. How am I going to say to a client, "You need a little epizeuxis"?

But who cares about the names? It is the potential impact that matters. I want to define just a few of them and give you examples that you can use immediately, whether you're talking or writing.

Figure of Speech	*Example*
Epizeuxis—repeating a word	"A mess. A mess. A mess. There's no other way to describe it."
Polypton—repeating a word, but the second use is in a slightly different form	"Let's think about this before we do something unthinkable."
Antanaclasis—repeating a word, but with two different meanings	"Until we get past this mess, we'll be living in the past."
Anaphora—repeating a word at the beginning of two or three lines	"Bad decision. Bad timing. Bad outcome."
Epistrophe—repeating a word at the end of two or three lines	"It was a lie. She was caught in the lie. I got stung by the lie."
Symploce—repeating the beginning and ending of the line	"They are a terrific client. They will always be a terrific client."
Epanalepsis—repeating the beginning at the end	"Our trust was rewarded with trust."
Anadiplosis—repeating the end of one line at the beginning of the next	"I thought it was a great idea, and a great idea was precisely what we needed."
Gradatio—repeating anadiplosis	"I thought it was a good idea, and good ideas are hard to find. And every good idea we found created another good idea in turn."

Congeries—heaping words with similar meanings on top of each other

"It was worked, tweaked, fiddled, and forced."

Antimetabole—repeating words in reverse grammatical order

"Less obvious is that we lost purchasing power, and purchasing power cannot be lost."

5

SO SMART, BUT LOOKS LIKE HE LACKS EXECUTIVE PRESENCE

Now that you have the juicy Chapter Four information about *sounding* composed, I want to turn my attention to *looking* composed— looking like someone with executive presence or, as some call it, presidential demeanor. The topic deserves its own chapter.

Looking Composed

First, I'll list the nonverbal variables that really count when people measure your composure:

- The way you touch others
- The way you use time
- Your facial expression
- The way you move your body
- The way you dress and groom yourself, *and* your body size
- The way you decorate your space

The most critical suggestions for looking composed and presidential are those related to touch, time, facial expression, body movement, and dress and grooming.

Touch

Your handshake, without exception, must convey confidence. If the grip is weak, it sends an unmistakable poor impression. The firmness of your grip and the length of the shake are sure signs of confidence and determination. Here's a story that genuinely and positively affected the life of my son, Matt, and it's all about a handshake. This happened when he was six years old.

Fess Parker owns a winery in the Santa Inez Valley near Santa Barbara, California. Our family drove there one weekend in 1996. Those of you who were born after 1960 may not know that Fess Parker, before becoming a real estate and wine tycoon, played the role of Davy Crockett in a Disney television series and motion picture—that is, unless your mother or father played videotapes of the shows for you, which is precisely what I had done for Matt. He came to love the character. Davy Crockett is an American icon. Fess Parker is pretty close to one himself.

Fess often spends Sundays at the winery. The day we went, we joined a line of visitors waiting for him to autograph a bottle of his Chardonnay. My son was standing in front of me. When Fess shook Matt's hand, Fess's facial expression signaled his disappointment. He said, "Son, I'm a-gonna show you how to shake a man's hand." He told Matt, "When I was a freshman at Texas A & M, I had to stop and shake the hand of every upperclassman who I met in the street. I had to walk over to him, stick out my hand, and say, 'Sir. I'm Fess Parker. I'm a-pleased to meet you.' And if'n he was with a young lady, you had to take off yer hat and say, 'It's a pleasure, ma'am.' And Matt, you had to really grip the feller's hand. So grip my hand right now and promise me you'll always do it just that way."

Even today, Matt tells anyone who asks that Davy Crockett taught him how to shake hands properly. I was a little embarrassed to have Davy find out that I hadn't done a good enough job.

Time

When people sit back and think about your executive presence, they cannot help but ponder whether you control time or are controlled by it. If you come across as frantic, as rushing from one meeting to another, you risk the perception among your colleagues that you haven't properly prepared for the day. I've heard clients described as the white rabbit in *Alice in Wonderland*. They're always saying, "I'm late, I'm late, for a very important date. I've got to go. I've got to run. I'm late, I'm late, I'm late."

If you start to fall behind on delivery dates, it will be noticed and racked up as a sign of lacking control. If you arrive late to meetings, it comes across not only as lacking control but also as disrespectful. But hold that thought, because we tackle it in Chapter Eight.

Here's a research result that is very thought provoking. People who speak very, very fast come across to seminar audiences as somewhere between youthful and immature. Speakers who are slower in delivery are considered thoughtful and mature.

Think about the message that you would want to convey to a prospective employer who told you that you would get a 3:00 P.M. phone call with the result of your interview. When the phone rings at precisely 3:00, would you pick it up immediately? Wouldn't you worry that it would appear you were hovering over the phone? Of course you would. You would wait for the phone to ring a second time, maybe a third, before picking it up. You would want to communicate a calm presence. That's your instinct kicking in and telling you to use time wisely.

Facial Expression

Whenever someone says, "She looked a little nervous," there's a 70 percent chance that her face shows it. As we will soon discuss, there is a possibility that you can also see nervousness in her posture, but nothing "jumps off your body" like your facial expression.

It has been said about body language in general—and this goes double for facial expression—that if there is a conflict between the message expressed in the words and the message that comes through in your body language or on your face, the latter message is going to prevail. Here are some examples.

When you are talking, your eyebrows move. Typically, when you accent something in the message, your eyebrows will move up on your face. Observers will read your degree of composure in that movement. When I first thought about writing *So Smart, But . . .*, I smiled at the thought of suggesting a person "move his or her eyebrows up." But there you are. It makes a huge difference.

Your eyes have more influence on your listener than your mouth does. The person you're talking to will judge your credibility when he or she watches your eyes as you get to the end of a thought. You can look over them, past them, or around them as a sentence unfolds. But you have to be looking at them as the sentence ends. Regarding your mouth, smiling is not the shining path to credibility. I recently read that a comedian suggested to John Kerry as he was running for the presidency in 2004, "If you're feeling good, tell your face." Kerry's reputation was that of a guy who was losing some credibility because he looked so serious while campaigning. I would have said, "Senator Kerry, your eyes look blank or vacant when you're talking and most especially as you get to the end of a thought. The comedian is saying 'tell your face.' I'm telling you to 'tell your eyes.' "

The Way You Move Your Body

There are so many settings, so many situations in which our body movement can be observed. Whether you are standing to make a presentation, sitting and contributing in a meeting, or walking to a meeting, people are seeing you and assessing your credibility. Every situation in which you find yourself proves the adage, "You cannot not communicate."

Maybe a little self-talk is in order here instead of a stage direction or technical direction. *You have to walk, sit, and stand as if you belong.* As one client put it, "I sit at the table recognizing that I have earned a place at the table." Close your eyes and imagine a picture of the president's cabinet as they meet in session. Whether they are talking or listening, the picture you have is of all of them sitting forward, hands clasped on the table.

Any added movement, any jerky movement, any touching of your face or rubbing of your hands on your arms or thighs will signal a loss of composure. I always imagine the look of Marlon Brando playing the Godfather as he sits in his chair in his study. In one classic scene, the only movement is in his hands as he pets a cat resting on his lap. Brando's intent is to convey the Godfather's power through controlled movement.

Of course I want you to learn about credibility through reading this book. But talking about Brando reminds me that I also want you to treat your study of credibility as a lifelong observation of popular culture. Think of it as Credibility 101: Appreciation of Credibility as Shown in Popular Culture. One important part of the "syllabus" is to watch the body movement of your local weatherperson on television. You might be lucky enough to see the proper body movement of a PowerPoint presenter. Figure 5.1 is a picture of my local

Figure 5.1. The Weatherperson.

weatherman. Imagine a PowerPoint slide behind him instead of the weather map.

The Way You Dress and Groom Yourself

I have chosen three stories about clothes and grooming (from a collection of more than three hundred stories I've personally experienced) to share with you. These are the ones that make communication consulting such a terrific career.

Before I tell them, I want to remind you that *the people who are judging you think you ought to be like them. And the organization you work for thinks you should be a good fit.* In the case of clothes, the word "fit" is a double entendre. You just have to look around. And if you say to yourself, "I ought to be able to dress the way I want to. The important question is whether I can do the work," I suggest you open your own business. Then you'll be the one doing the judging.

It's unfortunate that the dress rules are not clear. These days, the military is probably the only organization that explicitly tells you and shows you how to dress, how long to wear your hair, and how much jewelry you can wear. Everywhere else, you're working with an unwritten code. You're expected to "get it." Some people think the organization should set down the rules for the employees to follow. But the people who run the organization believe that any employee with half a brain could look around and get a sense of what fits and what does not fit.

Make no mistake, this material belongs right here in our discussion of composure, because clothes, grooming, and jewelry can express a certain level of control. If your shirt is flopping out of your pants: no control. If your hair is long and tangled: no control. If your socks have flopped down to your ankles: no control.

If you deliberately risk your credibility, the most precious possession you will ever have, over the way you dress, you do not belong in a corporate setting. Now I didn't say you would automatically lose your credibility. You may be extraordinarily lucky and work in a setting that places no judgments on dress and grooming. But when that setting changes, keep your eyes open.

The Case of the Hairy Lady

This story is from 1990. Given today's environment, it might not have happened as I'm going to describe it to you. Remember, though, that my intent is only to reinforce the point that people want you to match up to their expectations.

Ellen was a sophisticated, recently minted MBA with a mild disposition. Her boss told me that she had placed second in the latest round of interviews for a position in public affairs. In fact, she had placed second in three previous tries. When I asked him if he knew what the problem was, he said, "I can't really tell you. You meet with her and see if you can spot the problem." Maybe he knew and didn't want to tell me for fear that he would come across as shallow. That's not unusual.

She was seated at her desk when I was taken to her office. When she started to stand, I said, "Please," and motioned to her that it wasn't necessary to stand. She was pleased that the company had offered my services as a resource. I thought she would be a perfect fit for public affairs and a variety of other positions. Nothing jumped out at me.

We made plans to meet again. Then she got up and moved around the desk to escort me out. I immediately noticed that her legs were not shaved. Now maybe you're wondering, "Why were you looking at her legs?" I didn't have to look. They yelled up at me. She had a *lot* of hair on her legs. I hesitated at the door; I turned to her and said, "Let's sit down." I remember saying to my wife when I returned home that night, "In some situations, I don't get paid enough to say the kinds of things I have to say."

I gently told her that it was my impression that the hair on her legs was the reason she was passed over. I encouraged her to wear slacks or consider shaving her legs. I told her that the interviewers probably felt that it would send the wrong message to some of their customers. Of course, no one would own up to that because of the HR implications.

Ellen was utterly bewildered. She said that if I was right—and we didn't know for certain, it was just an educated guess—she didn't know if she would want to work there. She wasn't angry with me. In fact, she said it took a lot of courage to put it to her as I did.

I felt that the message she was sending might border on "too political" in that environment. At that time, hair was used, some felt, as a way of expressing a woman's right and responsibility to assert herself. Ellen told me that politics had nothing to do with it. She said, "My husband prefers a natural look."

She thought through it, talked with her husband, and decided that the job was worth keeping, that she would sacrifice a personal preference. Two months later, she was promoted.

The Case of the Overly Casual Friday

Do you remember Larry from Chapter Three? He was the fellow who told his boss, Bill, not to be so worried. In addition to missing the mark there, Larry didn't dress too well either. Not long after Larry and I started working together, Bill called me. He said, "As long as the two of you are meeting, here's something else about Larry that bugs me. While it's true that we have casual dress around here, he has taken casual to an extreme. He wears sneakers, and I'm not a fan of sneakers, but at least he could keep them clean. He wears jeans, and I'm not a fan of jeans either, but at least he could keep them pressed. He wears polo shirts because we do have a rule against T-shirts. But I keep my polo shirts crisp and neat. His shirts look old, crumpled, and nasty."

So Larry, who was already getting feedback about his priorities, was about to hear that he looked as though he had slept in his clothes. (You might be asking yourself, "Why don't people be up-front with their direct reports? Why don't they say what is on their mind?" I don't know the answer for all of them. I do know that it's a lack of will, a lack of skill, or a little of both.)

When we met, Larry said, "You know, Allen, I used to be Bill's boss. He leapfrogged me a couple years ago. I think I've subconsciously rebelled by looking so different from him. But I get the message." Larry made a pretty quick turnaround with his clothes, and that implied a more positive attitude.

The Case of the Yucky Hair Transplants

In 1984, I was asked to meet with a Human Resources director. He was looking for a coach to bring in for a number of possible executives, and my name was offered as a possibility. A couple of weeks before the meeting, I had gone in for hair transplants. And in those days, let's just say the micrograft technique had not been perfected. The fellow noticed that my forehead looked a little odd. Before you say, "Why in the heck did you go in for the meeting?" I'll tell you that I'm generally a risk taker and simply felt I could get away with it. A week went by. I called the fellow who'd recommended me and asked him if he'd heard anything about the meeting and how I'd come across. He said, "They're not going to use you. He felt that you were a 'Beverly Hills' type." Hair transplants were not as common as they are now, so my having gotten them signaled that I was "not their type of consultant." I should have known. They were a computer technology organization. Do you remember the adage "The best coaches were not always the best players"? That's my explanation for this mistake and a few others.

The Way You Decorate Your Space

Not long ago, I took my colleague Mike to a client meeting. He isn't an associate at CDA. He has his own consulting firm, but I often ask him to work with me on projects. We drove down to San Diego to meet with a woman who wanted to work on her credibility as a result of some feedback she had received.

When we were taken into her office, Mike immediately said, "You must be into feng shui and Far Eastern philosophy." You could have knocked me over with a feather. And she looked at him as if Confucius himself had just walked in. (Feng shui, developed by the Chinese thousands of years ago, is a guide to the arrangement of a home or workplace.)

Mike told her that he got the impression from two clues in her office. One, that she had turned her desk at an angle instead of positioning it parallel to the walls and, two, that she had a small rock arrangement on the desktop.

Regardless of whether or not Mike had pegged this client accurately, this story is a good example of the impressions you make on the people around you.

If you want to send a signal that you have executive presence, that you are someone who is very composed under pressure, what would you have in your office and hang on the wall? Here are some examples:

Pictures of you with politicians

Pictures of you climbing El Capitan

An organized desktop

College degrees

Leather-bound books

Civic awards

I may not have it exactly right, but the point remains—and always bears repeating: you cannot not communicate; there's a message in all we say and in all we do.

So Smart, But Presents Poorly

I need to explain my sense of how presentational speaking fits in the fabric of this book.

If you read contemporary academic research about credibility, you'll soon discover that scholars don't single out stand-up speaking for special consideration. Oh, you might pick up one of thousands of books on presentational speaking, but the advice, for instance, on making eye contact is the same as it would be if you were sitting one-on-one with a subordinate in your office. If you were a student, you would realize immediately that even though your classes might be divided by situation—public speaking, small group communication, interpersonal communication, health care communication, customer service communication, for example—the advice is always the same, meaning that the behavioral suggestions would be similar if not identical. In other words, advice about using a confident voice as a public speaker should be pretty close to the advice about using a confident voice in customer service.

Nevertheless, it's not uncommon for our consultancy to receive requests to conduct seminars with titles like "Executive Presentation Skills." Given that, I want to do my best to discuss any of the issues that could be unique to stand-up speaking. (Malcolm Kushner, who has written extensively on this subject in two books for Wiley Publishing under the Dummies imprint, remains my recommendation for more extensive study on the topic.) The next sections address the most common complaints and how to fix them easily and quickly.

If She's Just Going to Read the Slides, She Might as Well Just Sit Down and Let Us Read Them

You must, must, must have eye contact while you're speaking. The eye contact must, must, must come at the *end of most of your sentences.* By "end of the sentence" I mean the last three or four words. Even if you are not as familiar with the slide(s) as you'd like, you have to learn how to fake it till you make it.

Take a look at this list, which represents the content of a PowerPoint slide. I have highlighted some of the words by underscoring them. That is where you have to turn around and face the audience, or someone in the audience.

Arguments Supporting Our Position

- We can reduce your costs substantially without sacrificing quality.
- We can increase the speed of completion to ensure meeting your deadline.
- We can provide highly trained specialists to fill every position.
- We can provide training and development for each skill level.
- Our legal team will ensure accurate interpretation of appropriate regulations.
- We maintain the highest possible ethical standards.

I'm not suggesting that your slide should actually show the highlighting. The highlights are your reminder to turn around and face the audience. To pull this off naturally, you need to keep the bullet points you display *short*, maybe ten words or less. The longer the bullet point, the odder it will seem to the audience as they watch you read it.

I've traditionally explained the crucial importance of eye contact at the end of a sentence by pointing out that the end of a sentence has all the important content. If you look back at the list, you can see that "without sacrificing quality" and "meeting your deadline," for example, clearly deserve eye contact. You would trivialize the importance of these ideas if you were looking at the screen while you said the words. The fact is, any situation—stand-up, sit-down, or lay-down—offers the opportunity for you to emphasize an important point by having eye contact where it belongs. It's not enough for a facilitator of a presentation skills seminar to say, "You need more eye contact." It's the *timing* of the eye contact that matters.

If He Continues to Walk Around That Much While He's Presenting, I'm Going to Get Nauseated

Here's the rule about how much you should move while you're presenting: like a tree, the trunk stays in the ground and the limbs move. Get it? Generally speaking, you stand still—and pretty close to the image, by the way—while your arms do the gesturing. As I advised earlier, watch your local weatherperson. Watch how he or she stands reasonably still during the broadcast. The Weather Channel professionals are the least expensive and most reliable models for good stand-up speaking.

Her Manner Reveals No Passion for Her Work

Speak as if they're hard of hearing. You have to use a significantly louder voice than feels "normal." You cannot judge the appropriate volume by asking yourself how much volume you need in order to be heard. You have to ask yourself, "How much volume do I need to sound passionate about this?" You can't just say, "Can everyone in the back of the room hear me?" You have to say to yourself, "I want to convince everyone in the room how I feel about this, and that is going to take more volume than feels comfortable to me." Now, before you say, "That's crazy. I don't want to come across as a loudmouth aggressive research chemist," I'll tell you that yes, you can take anything to extremes and experience the resulting down-side. (I talk more about this in Chapter Eleven.) But trust me, you can really push the envelope on volume before someone will say, "Tone it down, Wally."

I Don't Know Which to Watch

In an advertising course I took as an undergraduate, I learned that billboards are designed with this in mind: a celebrity and the product she's hawking should be contiguous, or close together in space. That is, a driver speeding by the billboard should be able to connect the celebrity's face to the product she's hawking.

The way the rule applies in stand-up presentations is this: you have to stand closer to the image than to the LCD that's resting at the edge of the conference table. If you stand closer to the LCD than to the image you're projecting, the audience will either (1) focus on you to the detriment of the slide or (2) focus on the slide to your detriment. Once again, don't forget to watch the Weather Channel (and refer back to Figure 5.1). Those weatherpeople have this down pat.

There's Too Much Material on the Slide

"This slide is a little busy, but bear with me." How many times do you suppose someone said this today while showing an audience the organization chart with seventy-six boxes and names? How many times today has someone shown a slide with ten different reasons why their company should be chosen for the job and then verbally restated all ten? And how many times has someone displayed all ten reasons using PowerPoint's Reveal feature as if that were going to "do the trick"? Even if there's a reasonable justification for all that content on one slide, audiences are primed to complain about it.

So how do you deal with these situations? On the slide with the seventy-six boxes and names, you have to say something like this: "I thought it was important to show you the size of this organization, but I want to call attention to three names that you'll need to know in the short term." And it would help if those three boxes were highlighted. There's real value in showing the quantity of names to give a sense of the size of the organization. There is no value in remarking about many more than three of them.

Now, as to the slide with the ten benefits: It might look like this:

Our Company Offers Ten Specific Benefits

- Talent
- <u>Multiple Locations</u>
- Vast Experience
- Proven Reliability
- Industry Awards
- Blah
- Blah Blah
- Blah Blah Blah
- Blah Blah Blah Blah
- Even More and Blah

Don't read through all ten as a list, one item after another. But it doesn't hurt to show all ten. After all, you've got some bragging rights. You need to say something like, "I've laid out ten significant reasons for choosing us for this project. I'd like to call your attention to one of them" (maybe two). Highlight it, as I have here. "We have locations throughout the world. That gives us the ability to perform faster with lower cost, while maintaining maximum quality standards. For instance, the fact that you are aiming at the Virgin Islands and we have a Caribbean location makes us a logical choice." In other words, you go into a little depth on one as opposed to simply reading all ten. C'mon, you know that doesn't work when *you're* in the audience.

Finally, a word about using PowerPoint's Reveal feature. It's not a slam dunk no matter how fancily you can get each item to spin onto the slide. The audience can get very antsy if they don't know how much content you intend to reveal and have to wait until each separate item shows up. Their stress level is going up if they are starting to think something like *Holy moly, if his first bullet point has a font as small as that, who knows how many bullets he intends to reveal? We'll be here all day!* In the previous example, instead of using Reveal, you would do better to show all ten reasons at once and be more skilled in the way you talk through them.

A Final Thought About PowerPoint

Think about the term *visual aid*. PowerPoint slides were intended to be a visual aid to help people see something that words alone couldn't do justice to, couldn't fully describe. PowerPoint has also been justified on the grounds that some of us are "visual learners."

But words on a slide are not a visual aid. Words on a wall don't add value to the words heard from the speaker's lips. How many of your ministers and rabbis use PowerPoint in church? How many times have you seen a U.S. president use PowerPoint when he addressed the nation or the Congress? Never. A PowerPoint slide with a photograph, a plain old graph, or an architectural rendering makes sense. Those are clearly an aid. They help the audience see something that words fail to describe.

There's no getting around it, though: many attendees at meetings want a printed deck, want that deck projected on the wall, and want you to present the deck orally. So you have to learn to make PowerPoint presentations and make them well. But we all know they're a ritual without a lot of value . . . when they're just words on the wall.

And as to the "visual learners" thing, why don't people bring PowerPoint to the company lunchroom for one-on-one conversations with visual learners? How can people talk to a visual learner in the car? How do moms and dads have serious conversations with their "visual learner" kids about alcohol and drugs without Power-Point? It's ludicrous. Just because consultants say it's so doesn't make it so—unless it's me, of course.

6

SO SMART, BUT THINKS HE KNOWS IT ALL

I think about the character dimension of the credibility framework a lot. I fret over making judgments about my clients' integrity or morality or ethical choices. Maybe it's because I wouldn't want someone to make hasty judgments about me. I *do* know that I'd want people to say, "Weiner, he's a good guy." This chapter is a description of what I believe people mean when they say, "He's a good guy," and how it shapes perceptions of credibility. And by the way, there isn't an exact description in English for women that gets to the same meaning. Try saying "She's a good girl" to yourself and you'll realize in a heartbeat that it just . . . doesn't . . . work. Try "She's a great gal." Maybe "She's a fine person."

In *Human Communication*, Burgoon, Hunsaker, and Dawson (1994, p. 42) write, "The popular rejoinder 'You're a good man, Charlie Brown,' is an estimate of character perceived as goodness, decency, or trustworthiness." Here's another statement that says so much about perceived similarity and how much it determines credibility: "Many people will terminate conversations or avoid situations in which they might be forced to communicate with someone who *does not meet their personal standards of character*" (p. 43, emphasis added).

In our practice, we've heard a lot of thought-provoking comments on perceptions of character. Here is a partial list:

Arrogant	"Needs to be less full of herself."
Condescending	"Needs to treat us as equals."

Terrible listener	"Needs to stop multitasking."
Closed-minded	"Needs to open his mind to other possibilities."
Petty	"Needs to concentrate on the big things."
Micromanages	"Needs to trust our judgment."
Won't delegate	"Needs to let go so others will learn."
Doesn't trust others	"Needs to believe in us."
Not worthy of my trust	"Needs to be open and honest."
Slick	"Needs to get real. Comes across as totally artificial."
Rude	"Needs to show courtesy."

If you keep in mind that underlying each of these comments is the thought, "does not meet my personal standards of . . .," you will be reminded that we like, respect, and want to work with people who are like us. And when it comes to character, they typically think of themselves as warm and open.

In his recent book, *Politics Lost,* Joe Klein (2006) writes this about character:

> Character is one of the most overused and under-analyzed words in American politics. Let's attempt a simple definition: character is the intersection of beliefs and humanity. Beliefs are not policies; they are more fundamental than that—a coherent and accessible worldview. And a convincing demonstration of humanity involves more than photo ops at the state fair; it always involves some form of spontaneity. Usually a convincing humanity is the most important quality that a politician can bring to the table: in every election of the television era—with the exception of the Nixon elections—the "warmer" candidate has beaten the "colder" one. But in Reagan's case there was an odd inversion: the strength and clarity of his beliefs was the key to his success. . . .

Oh, the likability was surely there—but for Reagan, that aspect of his character was . . . his 'character.' That is, the character he played: his brilliant interpretation of what a president of the United States should *look and sound* [emphasis mine] like [p. 79].

Although this chapter is devoted to talking about the notions I've listed earlier, I need to explain something before going on. As terrible as it is to come across to people as arrogant, it serves no good to go to the other extreme and come across as exceedingly humble or literally without an opinion. If your colleague says, "What do you think?" you aren't helping anyone if you say, "Oh, whatever you think is all right with me. I don't have an opinion." But if you think of humility as the quality of realizing that someone else has a better idea than yours, it reveals your understanding of character.

Our firm fields many calls for seminars and coaching on the character issue. The complaint can be as subtle as "He doesn't tip the waiter," or as obvious as "He doesn't even nod his 'hello' when you pass him in the hall," but the truth remains that people can easily lose the credibility they've worked so hard to build. I cannot think of any single cluster of issues that can so derail a career as this one. And if you are asking yourself, "Can a tiger change its stripes?" I will tell you, "Yes. Without a lingering doubt."

Is it easy? No. It's a chore to change any kind of behavior. Ask a dieter. But you will read stories and suggestions in this chapter that will fill you with hope for the success of people who work with you and for you.

Late last year, I started consulting in a relatively small organization where many of the people were stressed out over the behavior of a new finance executive, Jim. One of the most interesting comments I heard at the start of the work was, "We've been a feminine organization. He's come in here with a macho attitude, and I've begun to think I made a huge mistake [hiring him]." The speaker was one of the owners, and she had about had it with this guy.

I didn't know precisely what she meant by a "feminine" organization. It turned out that she used that word to describe a level of politeness that they had historically treasured. People were used to asking for things ("Have you had a chance to finish that yet?") and walking very carefully around negative feedback ("I know you've had a lot on your plate, and all of us commiserate with what you're going through, but it would really help if you could begin delegating more of your duties to Anne.") Jim was saying, "Get that done. I can't believe you haven't finished." And he might say, "This is the last time I'm going to tell you to train Anne before I write you up."

When I met with Jim and began talking to him about the impression he was making (it just goes to show you how carefully they walked around negative feedback that they wanted *me* to talk with him), he said he was simply doing what they told him to do. He said his mandate coming in was to change things and get people "off their butt."

There are two takeaways from this story. One is the reminder, repeated throughout this book, that you have to come across reasonably close in style to the people who are judging you. Even if they tell you they want a different atmosphere, violating that principle will spell failure. Second is the broader message about change management. People have to be comfortable with you before they'll trust you to lead change. This goes back to what Frank Sinatra said about planning a live performance, as I mentioned in Chapter Three: before you can introduce your audience to new songs or new styles of singing, you first need to make them comfortable by singing their favorites as they remember them. I told Jim that unless he took Sinatra's advice, he was doomed and targeted for dismissal.

One other part of this story bears on the "Sinatra Rule." This organization mandates that personal mail not be sent to its address. After the mailroom received a piece of Jim's personal mail, he was reminded about the rule and asked to have it sent to his home. He refused. He required that the rule be changed to accommodate his needs. If ever there was an example of violating the Sinatra Rule, this was it. No matter how skilled you are, no matter how smart you are, you cannot bring this level of personal stress into an organization and hope to succeed. Jim left a month later.

By the way, whenever I'm asked how successful our firm is with our coaching engagements, I typically say we have a .700 batting average. The 30 percent of clients who don't demonstrate enough change to create positive impressions are not lacking skill. They are lacking sufficient will to work on themselves. My most successful clients have an ongoing curiosity and inquisitiveness about credibility and begin studying others to learn what will work for them. They don't magnify the issue beyond what it deserves, and they don't trivialize the issue below what it deserves.

Last year, a man I'd worked with ten years before passed away. He had a heart attack. He was, maybe, forty-two years old. When I met him, he was a management consultant for what must be the country's most famous management consulting firm, but he went on to become the CEO of a global corporation.

I met him as one of forty very senior management consultants enrolled in one of our company's credibility coaching engagements. In fact, it was called Managing Competence and Credibility.

As I always do, I sought and received feedback about him from his colleagues and clients. There was a theme to their comments. He was described as lacking a "counselor's manner." I told him that although of course a gifted management consultant has to be solid in his client's business, he must also have a personal manner and style that clients will be attracted to. The word "counselor" evokes a softer footprint than the phrase "management consultant." Doesn't it to you? I told him that a counselor has a sound and a look. As a counselor, you speak your words more thoughtfully so that your client will reflect on them. Your volume might be a little lower than normal so that your client reads more feeling into your words. I modeled some examples.

He reamed me a brand new ear canal. He was livid! He told me I didn't belong there. I didn't, in other words, belong in such a sophisticated work environment if that was the extent of my contribution. He stormed out of the room and never came back. Whatever. It wasn't the first time and wouldn't be the last.

His intellect served him well enough for him to leave consulting and move into a senior leadership position. But his reputation for not being a "people person" dogged him throughout his tenure. Some people thought his death was a result of the stress of a high-powered position. Some people thought it was the accident of genes. But I always felt that his reactions, including his failure to stay centered when counseling and when listening to the counsel of others, was a contributing factor.

Does your attitude account for your behavior, or does your behavior determine your attitude? I argue for the latter. Yelling, screaming, face-turning-red outbursts cannot be good—unless your teenager comes home late. Then it's OK.

The Cure for Sounding Arrogant and Condescending

Remember from Chapter Two: how you sound when speaking and how you sound when listening both make an impression. We'll begin with the "when speaking" half.

Your Word Choice and Language Choice When Speaking

In *Human Communication*, Burgoon, Hunsaker, and Dawson (1994) write about *language expectancy theory*. In short, people develop social norms about language in a given situation. They expect certain things. We expect our spouse, friends, and coworkers to use a certain kind of language when they try to persuade us. Over time, the norms can be pretty rigid. If communicators violate a norm, violate a listener's expectations, the listener will not be as receptive. One factor in the equation is word choice or, more broadly speaking, language choice.

One aspect of language choice has to do with what is called *opinionated language*. When a speaker uses opinionated language, he communicates not only his attitude about the topic but also his attitude about those who agree or disagree with him. Sitting with your coworkers at a restaurant table at lunch, for example, you might say, "I think it makes sense to spin off that piece of the business." Stated that way, it's simply your opinion. But if you say, "Only someone who doesn't know the business would argue against spinning it off," you're using opinionated language, and you come across as arrogant. Even if you say something positive like, "Everyone who is familiar with this business knows that spinning it off is the right thing to do," you still risk being perceived as arrogant.

A second aspect of language choice that can have a negative effect on how you are perceived is called *language intensity*. This is the measure of the "distance between *your* point of view and a neutral position" (Burgoon, Hunsaker, & Dawson, p. 1994, 233). Let's go back to the restaurant. If you say, "That piece of the business is *destroying* our chances," it does not sound neutral. If you say, "That piece of the business is *causing us some real problems*," it has a neutral quality. "Destroying" is much, much more intense than "causing problems."

Qualifiers (and the lack of them) are another element of language intensity. Using them helps you express the right amount of probability and prevents your coming across as arrogant. Again, back to the restaurant at lunch. Let's let someone else do some talking. One of your colleagues says, "There's no question that a spin-off is the right thing to do." Another one says, "I think *perhaps* you're right." A third person says, "I'm going to vigorously suppress the idea." A fourth colleague says, "Paulie is *probably* going to frown on that." The words that express slightly less certainty, at least a hint of probability, will sound less arrogant.

As you might guess, metaphors with violent connotations are very intense and therefore risky when it comes to seeming arrogant. Now we're leaving the restaurant and walking back to work. Joe says, "No matter who comes out on top, it will *suffocate* the workforce."

Marie adds, "I agree. The feeling I get is they've already been *brutalized* by senior management."

No book can make absolute conclusions about something as mercurial as arrogance. If you have a credible history, if you have been a producer and a rainmaker, you can get away with more intense language. But, in general, walk cautiously around these kinds of expressions.

Your Word Choice and Language Choice When Listening

As we've said, it's not hard to mistakenly sound arrogant through the way you express your point of view on a topic. But how about the way you react to someone else's point of view? The way you react is just as potentially troublesome as the way you act. Here are some sample reactions to the same statement. Say each pair to yourself. Ask yourself, "What would I rather hear?" Which reactions sound arrogant?

The sample statement is, "I think we should consider outsourcing that function. We would save a lot of money and get the job into the hands of people who really know what they're doing."

A. "That's an option I hadn't thought about."

B. "I'd already considered that."

A. "What's your thinking around it?"

B. "There's no need to go into that."

A. "Why do you think so?"

B. "Why would that help?"

A. "It makes a lot of sense."

B. "That makes no sense."

I believe you will agree that someone using choice B in every pair would be considered a "poor listener." In contrast, each choice A would leave you thinking, "She listened to me. She may not have agreed, but she was definitely listening." If you act as if you have made up your mind and do not have the time or patience to listen to the views of others, you will be labeled as arrogant. Trust me.

Before moving on, I need to share with you a fundamental truth about listening as a phenomenon of credibility. Listening has always been a very popular seminar and workshop topic. We have gathered hundreds of thousands of Essessnet comments about people who fail to listen. I need to clarify for you that very, very few of the people who accuse others of "not listening" are concerned that the listener will not remember what was said. If Ethan, commenting about Kathy, says, "Kathy just . . . does . . . not . . . listen," he is expressing his anger that Kathy is resistant to his point of view. *He is not angry about her ability to recall what he said the next day. Very few annoyed speakers are concerned about recall. They are angry about the listener's closed-minded attitude.*

If you've taken a listening seminar, you will recall hearing these kinds of suggestions to help you concentrate:

- Paraphrase: "If I understand you correctly, you're saying . . ."
- Reflect: "The look on your face is telling me . . ."
- Summarize: "OK. So we're decided three things . . ."

You were probably also encouraged to

- Eliminate distractions
- Look for key ideas
- Ask questions

Maybe all these techniques will help you recall the speaker's ideas. But if they are effective and you leave the speaker happy, it's because you've used them to make her feel more valued as a contributor.

The Way You Argue (When Speaking)

The rule here is so simple. You cannot tell other people why their view is wrong and still avoid sounding arrogant. And that arrogant message is made even worse when you tell them they are wrong in a public setting, as opposed to talking to them one-on-one.

No one likes to hear a message that sounds like, "You're wrong. It doesn't make sense." People don't mind it so much when you say, "I think I'm right about this." Which of these two statements would sound better to you if you were a Kerry supporter?

A. "George Bush will be a great president." (I'm right.)

B. "John Kerry will be a terrible president." (You're wrong.)

As distasteful as A might be to you, it is bound to sound better than B.

The cure for this most common form of arrogance is called the *two-sided message*. The basic premise is that your argument follows the form, "I'm right. You're right. On balance, I'm a little more right." Figure 6.1 is a model.

We'll follow Figure 6.1 to lay out a hypothetical argument in favor of George Bush's reelection as president. Start at the top of the diagram: *Your Viewpoint*. You might say, "George Bush should be reelected." Corresponding to the three boxes labeled *Subpoint*, you might say, "Number one, he's more experienced. Number two, he's stronger on homeland security. And number 3, he's succeeded in turning around the economy." The *Data Points* boxes symbolize your proof. And you better have some good proof. Remember, you need statistics and anecdotes to prove your points.

Now, moving to the next level, the box labeled *Opposing Viewpoint* symbolizes your saying, "*A case could be made* for John Kerry's candidacy." I've italicized "A case could be made" because it signals your

Figure 6.1. Two-Sided Message.

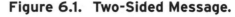

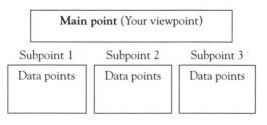

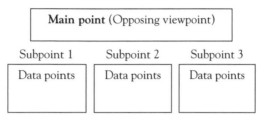

fair-mindedness on the issue. The following *Subpoints* boxes reflect the case for Kerry. You might say, "He comes to the job with a lot of foreign policy experience. Second, there's a belief that he will click with European leaders and get their cooperation to a greater extent than President Bush has; and third, he has a very strong running mate in John Edwards, who could also be trusted with the presidency."

But at the bottom, you come to the conclusion that supports your initial thinking. That last box symbolizes the words, "On balance, I think the arguments for President Bush are going to make him a winner."

Here is a whole statement without the explanatory comments:

I think George Bush should be reelected. For one thing, he's more experienced. He's also stronger on homeland security. And finally, he's doing a pretty good job turning the economy around. Now a case could be made for Kerry's candidacy. You're right that he comes to the job with a lot of foreign policy experience. And he may have a better relationship with European leaders and get more cooperation than President Bush has been able to get. And finally, he has a very strong running mate in John Edwards. He could be trusted with the presidency if necessary. But on balance, I think the case for Bush is the stronger case.

Compare that with, "I think George Bush should be reelected. Anyone who thinks John Kerry would make a good president is out of his gourd. He's a terrible communicator. He's a flip-flopper. And he didn't really earn those medals."

Your Tone of Voice

As I'm sure you will understand, it is very, very hard to portray voice qualities in print. There are a few, however, that I believe you will recognize as you read about them. Each section here includes examples. Say them to yourself and see if you agree with me.

Avoid Very Slow Delivery. All of us have our own delivery pace, a speed we use when we talk, and people who know us recognize it. People who know us very well know our voice so well that they can tell when something is odd or wrong. Your friends will say, "I can tell by your voice that something is bothering you."

Any violation of your normal pace will set off the listener's alarm bell. Speaking more slowly than usual is the most common violation that comes across as arrogant or condescending. Speaking too slowly leaves the impression, intended or unintended, that you believe that if you don't slow down, the listener won't "get it."

Recently I was in a doctor's waiting area when a patient approached the receptionist's window. She wanted to leave a package for the doctor, but she was clearly afraid that such a "low-level" employee as a receptionist might not be trustworthy. Instead of saying, "Would you be sure the doctor gets this," the woman said, "It . . . is . . . very . . . very . . . important that the doctor receives . . . this . . . package." She also used the term "dear," as in "receives this package, dear."

If you had not seen the woman, but just heard her speak, you would have thought she was talking to a ten-year-old—hence the word *condescending,* or talking down to.

Avoid Overly Pronounced Delivery.   One of my favorite words is *pedant* or *pedantic.* A pedant overrates the importance of trivial points. He or she is typically narrow-minded, and insists on sticking to a set of arbitrary rules—including self-imposed rules about pronunciation. If you try to pronounce all the consonants in your words, you risk sounding pedantic and condescending. I have said elsewhere that a bias towards consonants can add a tone of assuredness to your message. But this, as well as any technique taken to extremes, has a downside and pedantry is the downside here.

Recently I approached the agent at an airline ticket counter. I handed him my printout of the Internet reservation. The agent smiled and began looking at his computer screen while looking for my record. I am no doubt revealing my own prejudices here, as I travel so much, but surely all of you reading this have had a similar experience. The agent looked up and said, in a normal voice tone, "I can't find your reservation. I'm sorry, but I'll have to rebook you on the next available flight."

I said, "Can you look once again? The confirmation number is on that paperwork."

The agent looked at me, eyeball to eyeball, and said, "SSSir. Azz I toldd you once before, we do nott have a recordd of you making a reservation."

I was not a happy camper. I looked right back at the agent and said, "Cannnn You Findddd Ittttt?" Bad behavior is contagious. (By the way, I waited for the next flight.)

Avoid Using Monotone. What About Polytone?   If you have ever taken a seminar on presentation skills, you have heard a facilitator describe a speaker as having a monotone. Speaking in monotone is probably the most commonly cited "problem" in presenters. Although it is certainly true that you risk putting people to sleep with dull content *and* a monotone, it is not as big an issue as you might think. The English language has only a few tones to work with: we have a tone to express surprise; we have a tone to ask a question; we might use a higher tone to emphasize a point. Asiatic languages have hundreds of distinct tones. We do not. So if a native English speaker starts to add more tones than usual to his speech, he can sound like a parody of a radio announcer—and sound condescending. Once again, this is tricky to depict in print, but it might sound like this if a presenter were to switch from monotone to what we'll call polytonal. I'll show the monotone first, followed by the polytonal version. Read the small capitals in the second version with a higher, perhaps questioning tone.

> Today I'm going to show you our revised plan. I'll start with the budget and then show you the updated milestone chart and finally introduce two new team members.

> ToDAAAY I'm GOYing to SHHHOW you our reVIIISED plan. I'LL start with the BUUUUDget and then show you the UUUUUPdated MIIIILEstone chart and FIIIINally introDOOOCE TWO NEW TEAM members.

If how I've written this conveys what I intended, the second version should sound like a kindergarten teacher talking to the class and not a manager talking to the team. It should sound condescending. *To condescend,* by the way, is defined as "to descend to the level, regarded as lower, of the person that one is dealing with; to deal with others in a patronizing manner" (McKechnie, 1983).

So Smart, But Looks "Cheesy"

Just as vocal tones can be overdone, so can gestures. People tend to perceive overdone and out-of-place gestures as cheesy. Your best shot for learning about this is to start looking for examples on television and in movies. I hope you will conclude, "Weiner was right about this. It does look cheesy." *Cheesy* is such a great word to describe this look, and I cannot take credit for it. I have heard it used to describe many, many people. But first some background on gesturing.

Nonverbal communication classes term the two types of gestures *illustrators* and *emblems*. An illustrator does just what it sounds like: it illustrates what you're saying. One example is holding your thumb to your ear and your index finger to your mouth to describe a phone conversation. Another one is clasping your hands with intertwined fingers to describe a team that is cohesive. Yet another might be forming fists, fingers toward your chest, working your hands back and forth like pistons to describe a team that is not "in sync." You might see Tony Robbins doing this kind of gesturing in front of twenty-five thousand people in a large auditorium and think it looks terrific. But in a conference room with six people, it looks cheesy. And cheesy is awfully close to artificial. And artificial is dangerously close to phony. And phony is cheesy. So stop it.

The only gestures that look "normal" while still showing a certain passion are the ones called emblems. Emblems show your enthusiasm through the movement of your hands, but your hands aren't forming visual descriptions of the words the way your middle finger can express your opinion about another driver. Picture yourself standing in your backyard in the summer talking with someone. You are both holding a beverage—a Corona beer maybe. You are holding it in front of you with both hands. When you start to speak, you will move your hands apart. We call that movement a "basketball" because it looks as if you've just passed a basketball to someone. That gesture is the simple key to the kingdom of looking sufficiently animated while you are talking. It sounds weird but look for it when you watch news anchors talking while they are standing.

The Cure for Looking Arrogant and Condescending

Arrogant body language is a bear to explain in print. One thing makes it easier: most of the offensive body language emerges *when a person is listening,* not when he or she is talking. We'll look at both situations, though.

So Smart, But Looks Odd When She's Listening

I want to start with the unintentional signals you might send while you are listening to someone else, because as I said, these tend to be the most irritating to others. It is very, very possible for someone to leave you, walk back to his office, and say to a third person, "That guy has a way about him that I can't put my finger on, but it just bugs me." I could describe many, many of these, but I'll limit my descriptions to the top seven offenders.

1. If you are the senior person and you are sitting at your desk, do not put your feet up on your desk. The nonverbal message is, "I can get comfortable, but you can't."

2. If you *continually* nod as the other person speaks, the nonverbal message is, "I'm not agreeing with you, but I want to show you just how passionate I am about your trivial little topic and I've been to a seminar where this technique was taught."

3. If you don't nod *at all* as the other person speaks, the nonverbal message is, "I'm not going to give you the pleasure of even the smallest response. After all, if I nod, you'll think I agree with you. And that's not the case."

4. If you look behind the speaker—say, at a basketball game on the TV behind the bar—the message is, "You're fine, but basketball is better."

5. If you tap your fingers on the table top, if you bang out a rhythm with a pencil, the message is, "Get on with it, please."

6. If you rock back and forth in your desk chair, the message is, "Get on with it, please."

7. If you clear messages on your BlackBerry while someone is speaking to you, stop reading now. *So Smart But . . .* is a waste of your time.

Those are the big seven, but there are a couple of other ideas I want to mention.

If you don't sit squarely in your chair, the message is, "I'm halfway to getting up because I'm so bored."

A few years ago, I read a study about facial expression that made a very interesting claim. The authors suggested that some of us listen with our mouths closed—not tightly closed, but simply with our lips touching. The rest of us listen with our mouths slightly open—not open like someone sleeping or snoring on an airplane, but slightly open. Those with lips slightly open were perceived to be "more open to the speaker's message." You have to love that. Look for it in those who are listening to you. See if this makes sense.

A word on crossing your arms. Anyone who has ever read the book *Body Language*, by Julius Fast, or has taken a communication seminar sometime in the last thirty years, will claim that crossing your arms across your chest will make you look defensive or make you appear closed to the message you are hearing. The fact is that most of what people perceive about your attitude comes from your face and not your chest. If you present an open, friendly face while listening, it isn't crucial that you unfold your arms. On balance, is an open-armed look better than a crossed-armed look? Yes, it is. But it is *not* the determining factor; it's not the tipping point.

How You Look When Speaking

As far as looking arrogant or condescending *when you are speaking* is concerned, there are two main sources of really offensive behavior that clients tell us about or record in our Essessnet program for gathering 360° feedback. The first concerns eye contact, and the second has to do with posture.

When you are talking, it is vital—not just important but vital—that you reestablish eye contact at the end of every, or almost every, sentence. The ends of sentences are critically important moments in face-to-face communication. Think about it. In English, the juiciest parts of a sentence are at the end, not the start. Remember the order of things: subject, verb, object. Nothing can really compete in importance with the object. If you say, "I just don't think that he has the bandwidth for this kind of challenge," the meat of the thought is at the end: "the bandwidth for this kind of challenge." If you are looking up to gather your thoughts and begin to speak this thought, you need to refocus on your listener(s) once you get to the word "bandwidth." If you don't, you will risk coming across as lacking the energy or the will to make an important connection with your listeners.

As far as posture is concerned, you can't let your fatigue take over in such a way that you sit or stand too casually. The person talking with you wants to believe that his or her message is worthwhile enough to make you alert to its possibilities. When meetings begin, at say 8:00 A.M., most people sit up with their arms propped on the table. It's a way of showing that you are alert and "ready to roll." It's as if you're saying, "OK. I'm ready for the race to begin." If you are overly casual, your posture says, "I can't imagine anything you're saying being important enough to get me to sit up."

As I was writing this section, I had a conversation with a CEO about a COO with whom I've been working. His comments highlight some of what I've said here about character. He gave him a little praise and a little criticism. There were three items on the original "work order," including being more positive (composure), less intimidating (*character*), and displaying better judgment (competence). The CEO gave me a "well done." He said, "Charlie has made great strides in demonstrating a more positive attitude with his folks. I can hear how much difference it makes when he finishes on the positive. It was as if, using the language of couples, he had always said, 'I love you, but . . .' instead of 'but I love you.' It's made a huge difference."

He went on to say that Charlie had also shown a much less intimidating persona than before. The CEO noticed that Charlie's facial expression was much less stern while he listened, that he seemed inviting. He thought this was Charlie's biggest breakthrough.

He said, though, that there was still "work to do" on the character side. And, wouldn't you know it, he cited examples of odd judgment about things like coming in late, undisciplined e-mails, and expense statements that weren't quite right. I told him that I wouldn't be satisfied until that third item on the "work order" was satisfactorily completed. We've got some character building to do.

So Smart, But Doesn't Earn My Trust

The essence of trust is captured in the word *expectancy*. Can a person expect you to deliver on a promise? The promise could be your wedding vows. The promise could be a pledge you made to see that someone would be a candidate for promotion. As a kid, if all were going well, you would expect your dad to act like a dad every time he came home from work. You would expect your mom to act like a mom every time you got up and ready to go to school. You would expect your older brother to "have your back" if you were bullied. You would expect your older sister to defend you with your parents when you got into trouble.

Turning our attention to work, your colleagues (most of them, anyway) will give you a lot of latitude when it comes to depending on you. We all know that "stuff happens." You have to be careful, however, to avoid doing the same thing so often that it's attributed to your personality. You cannot violate expectations so often as to call into question someone's trust that you'll deliver on those expectations. It turns out to be a timing issue (the T in SMART, which I introduced in Chapter One). If you do anything—or fail to do anything—too many times, you create a huge risk that you'll be a marked person.

A Final Word About Character

The word *character* evokes images more profoundly consequential than some of the ones I've written about. I've concentrated on the issues brought most often to our firm by our clients and the ones we're trained to address.

President Clinton did not leave office under a dark cloud as a result of coming across as arrogant or condescending. No one ever accused him of being a poor listener. No, President Clinton left office with a dark cloud of doubt about his character as a result of adultery. *So Smart But . . .* has no suggestions for people who have left doubts about their character as a result of what you might call Ten Commandment sins. We do not tackle

1. So smart, but uses the Lord's name in vain.
2. So smart, but doesn't honor his mother and father.
3. So smart, but murders people.
4. So smart, but commits adultery.
5. So smart, but steals stuff.
6. So smart, but lies.
7. So smart, but covets the neighbor's husband or wife.

There's another classic book for those kinds of things.

7

SO SMART, BUT ISN'T A PEOPLE PERSON

"I don't care if they like me. They just have to respect me."

People who say that know they aren't liked and want to find a way to excuse it instead of working on it.

Two years ago, we began an engagement with a company in Texas. Bob, the fellow who championed the work, knew us from some coaching he had been involved with five years earlier, when he was with a different company. That organization put a lot of time and effort and money into offering coaching and seminars on a wide variety of topics. His current company was just beginning to see the potential benefits of outside advice and counsel on credibility issues.

Bob wanted ten people to be involved in the program. One of the participants was a woman from Finland. I mention Finland early in the story because she attributed much of her credibility "problem" to her fine country of birth. This is not at all unusual. I don't mean Finland, just the fact that people attribute idiosyncrasies to their homeland.

Bob told me that his team member was cold. He said she never said hello to anyone, no matter where she ran into them, and did not return a hello if expressed to her. "She doesn't mean it, and she doesn't realize it, but people notice it. It could definitely hurt her chances for promotion here because we're a pretty friendly culture."

As to Finland, the woman told me that her behavior was a cultural thing. She said that Finns, and Scandinavians in general, are not as outwardly expressive as Americans. In addition to blaming her native culture, she had a personal problem with American culture. She said, "I don't know why Americans put so much attention on being liked."

I explained that even if she thought the "real" reason for her behavior had to do with cultural differences, her colleagues didn't see it that way. They simply thought she was ignoring them. Look back at Chapter Three. You may attribute your behavior to things like "your culture." Your colleagues will attribute your behavior to your personality.

I introduced my early mentor, Jim McCroskey, at the start of this book. He fathered the studies on credibility and has some of the responsibility for naming the factors. He and others with whom he was studying originally named this factor *sociability*, as noted in the Introduction. He wrote that communicators who project likableness to their receivers are regarded as sociable (McCroskey, Hamilton, & Weiner, 1973, p. 44). I didn't like using the label "sociability," and my clients didn't like it either. So we renamed it Likability.

Basically, liked people tend to influence others more than those who are not liked. In fact, people who are liked are more credible than those who are not liked. The people we hang around with can shape and change our attitudes toward a lot of issues. Your peers actually have some influence on your political thoughts and your buying decisions, and, of course, you have influence on theirs—if you are liked.

Credibility research reveals that, while likability is the key, there are other important feelings involved than being likable. Even if your colleagues are not your friends per se, if they cooperate and act friendly on a work-related project, they will be perceived as more sociable. If you are friendly and cheerful, chances are that people will prefer being around you and working with you more than they would with someone who is unfriendly and grumpy. In short, unfriendly people will not be a part of our daily activities and, as a result, will not have a chance to be much of an influence on us.

One insight from the Myers-Briggs Type Indicator (MBTI) is the definition of *extroversion*. Many people think of an extroverted person as someone who is animated and outgoing. They think of someone who talks loudly and gestures a lot. If you have attended a public speaking seminar in recent years and the facilitator told you to "gesture more," you know what I mean. I write more about these qualities in Chapter Eight.

But the MBTI definition of extroversion is someone who "draws his or her energy from others." In short, that must be the feeling others get from your appearance. You have to show that you are not happy unless you reach out to others and they reach out to you.

What do I mean when I use the word "appearance"? I mean that no one has to know what you truly are; no one has to know that you draw even greater amounts of personal energy from being alone (that is, that you are introverted). Regardless of your true prefer-ence, you have to demonstrate the desire to be around others if you care about your overall credibility.

If I were to reduce all our knowledge about credibility into one word, I might choose *flattery*. I might claim that anyone who feels flattered by someone else's expression of interest will probably find that person credible. After all, if you are talking to someone who seems very interested in what you are talking about, you will feel flattered. That, in its essence, is at the heart of likability.

Sounding Likable

You know that all qualities emerge because someone sees them or hears them. Let's start with examples of sounding likable.

"What Do You Do on Weekends?"

Given that you're committed to "reaching out," people have to hear your expressions of interest in them and their families. It is really abominable that this kind of outward interest in someone else is called "small talk." Where in the world did that term come from? As if "big talk" existed. You should be asking your colleagues about themselves and their families.

I attended a seminar recently. After pairing the participants up, the facili-tator asked us to interview each other and then introduce our partner to the rest of the group. I asked my partner, "What do you do on Satur-days?" He was full of details. And I showed a lot of interest in things like his son's soccer game; the trips he makes to Sears for tools; the errands he runs for the family, including picking up dry cleaning and doing some grocery shopping; and his treating himself to a baseball game now and then. I asked him how he got into tools and whether he bases his choices on budget or quality. I asked him for advice about choosing a hacksaw for myself. He was really happy to be around someone who expressed an interest at such a detailed level, and I knew I had won him over. I wasn't even contributing that much talk time. I was spending most of the time listening. It makes me wonder more about the term *small talk*. Because I was mostly listening, was it "small listening"? Of course not. The time I spent listening resulted in his making a connec-tion with me that proved helpful in the course of the seminar.

Ask your colleagues, "What do you do on weekends?" It's a lot more inviting than, "Tell me about yourself."

"I Need Your Advice"

Everyone wants to feel needed. Even introverts enjoy feeling needed. And everyone has opinions. You need to ask your colleagues for their opinion or advice on any topic—especially topics you think you are expert in. It's extremely flattering to be thought of as a per-son with good ideas, and, of course, it's insulting to be thought of as a person with few valuable insights.

I especially like to ask my clients for advice on topics involving their professional expertise:

"Should I buy high-octane fuel? Does it really make a difference?"

"Should I buy branded drugs or generics? Does it really make a difference?"

"Is this the best time to think about refinancing my home loan?"

"Do you like your BlackBerry? Should I get one?"

"Do you like your laptop? Should I get one?"

I'm fond of saying, "One wonderful thing about consulting with a variety of clients in a variety of industries is that you get to be three paragraphs deep in so many topics. It really helps at cocktail parties when you are trying to connect with strangers." (More on "three paragraphs deep" later.)

I always tell myself, *Take advantage of the gift you've been given. Learn from your clients.* In addition, it's a terrific way to show Likability.

Stephen Miller has written a terrific book titled *Conversation: A History of a Declining Art.* I saw it profiled by Russell Baker (2006) in the *New York Review of Books.* Baker opens his review with his take on Mark Twain's *Huckleberry Finn* when Huck and Jim raft down the Mississippi. Baker writes: "Huck and Jim—and who could be less elite?—enjoy some of literature's memorable conversation by intuitively following principles laid down by masters of the art. Thus: Both participants listen attentively to each other; neither tries to promote himself by pleasing the other; both are obviously enjoying an intellectual workout; neither spoils the evening's peaceable air by making a speech or letting disagreement flare into anger; they do not make tedious attempts to be witty." I'm going to suggest Miller's book and Baker's review to all my clients whenever the likability issue comes up.

Talk About Your Foibles

Great word, *foible.* A foible is a small weakness. When I talk about mine, people talk about theirs. Sometimes that helps us make a connection. I think I've surprised a lot of people by my willingness to share a weakness, and it's helped them open up to me. The more "unsuitable" my weakness—to a point—the more I've invited such a connection. Most of the time, the person I've been talking with will say, "Don't be so hard on yourself. I can go you one better." I believe it has made me more likable and will do the same for you. Here are some examples from my experience:

> "I'm not great with other people's kids."
>
> "I'm impatient with waiting in line at Starbucks as people order complicated drinks."
>
> "People who yell into their cell phones in the airplane before takeoff bug me."
>
> "I spanked my son when he was little. Do you think it was a mistake?"

Tell Stories

Storytelling is a very attractive interpersonal skill. You open up so many possible avenues for making a connection when you do. The feeling your listener gets is something akin to "She must think I'm worth the effort, and that feels good. I like her." The stories do not have to be particularly self-disclosing to qualify as coming from a likable person. And they don't have to be clever. You don't have to read *Chicken Soup for the Soul,* with all its great anecdotes, to be a great storyteller.

A story has a beginning, middle, and end. It's better when there are characters in it and, even better, when you can hear the characters' voices. There are images in a story, and they are better when you describe them, when you paint pictures, so to speak. The beginning of an adult's story is almost exactly like a children's story beginning. A child's story starts with, "Once upon a time." Adult stories start with, "About a _____ ago," as in "About a year ago . . ."

Imagine sitting with your team at the start of a meeting. Your intention is simply to say, "All right, let's get started. I want to kick this off with a brainstorming session on best practices for customer service. Let's just go round the table. Jeff, you start." It's serviceable, all right. It saves time, you might say. It places task above the interpersonal imperative.

You could say instead, "You know, about a month ago I was talking with Fred Simmons in our finance department. We were on the same rental shuttle together at the airport in San Jose. He said to me, 'You know, Jim, if we don't get our act together, this is going to be a long year.' I think Jim's warning is accurate, and I want us to keep it in mind as we start brainstorming today. Jeff, why don't you kick it off."

Of course the stories can be more personal, and so much the better. Suppose at the same meeting you said, "Many years ago [once upon a time], my dad and I were talking about customers and their expectations. We were having a glass of cold milk at the Dairy Queen on a very hot summer day in Charleston, West Virginia. It was our regular Sunday outing. He said, 'You know, Allen, customers expect a lot, and they don't really care how you make it happen. I spend so many hours hand stitching a buttonhole so a jacket will look just right. I can't think of a time when a customer asked me about it. They have their own worries.' I think my dad was right, and it goes to the heart of our meeting today. Let's brainstorm our entire customer service enterprise and figure out ways to help them see how it's both detail oriented and effortless."

Of course, your stories *can* come from *Chicken Soup for the Soul*. The Chicken Soup books are full of anecdotes intended to make a point in an artful way. The stories have a way of depicting you as a warm, friendly person speaking from your "soul." Here's an example that you might use for the same customer service topic (Canfield, 1993, p. 22).

A friend of ours was walking down a deserted Mexican beach at sunset. As he walked along, he began to see another man in the distance. As he grew nearer, he noticed that the local native kept leaning down, picking something up and throwing it out into the water. Time and again he kept hurling things out into the ocean.

As our friend approached even closer, he noticed that the man was picking up starfish that had been washed up on the beach, one at a time, he was throwing them back into the water.

Our friend was puzzled. He approached the man and said, "Good evening, friend. I was wondering what you are doing."

"I'm throwing these starfish back into the ocean. You see, it's low tide right now and all of these starfish have been washed up onto the shore. If I don't throw them back into the sea, they'll die up here from lack of oxygen."

"I understand," my friend replied, "but there must be thousands of starfish on this beach. You can't possibly get to all of them. There are simply too many. And don't you realize this is probably happening on hundreds of beaches all up and down the coast. Can't you see that you can't possibly make a difference?"

The local native smiled, bent down and picked up yet another starfish, and as he threw it back into the sea, he replied, "Made a difference to that one."

After relating this story, you might say, "The story makes the point that every one of us, and every act of service we perform, might just make the difference for a customer. So let's think about that as we brainstorm the customer service function today."

The positive impact of storytelling on your reputation for likability is enormous.

Go Three Paragraphs Deep

The people around you like it when you can chat with them about topics they're interested in. If someone says, "My daughter and I went to the park Sunday. She got a model plane, and we went out and flew it," he or she will like the fact that you're interested in model planes. It makes the person feel good.

I have a general rule about this, which is to try to be three paragraphs deep on just about every subject. Most of the time it turns out I'm one paragraph deep, but I work on it. I read a lot because I want to, and I read a lot because it helps me connect with people. I read fiction and nonfiction. But more to the point of this section, I read trade papers, entertainment weeklies, financial news, hobby websites, and so on.

Not long ago, someone told me how much he likes roller coasters. Now that's pretty arcane. He talked about the history, the construction problems, and the biggest ones in the world. I told him how interesting I thought it was and how I knew there was a big one in Sandusky, Ohio. He launched into a whole riff on Sandusky. I didn't have to demonstrate that I was three paragraphs deep. I uttered one or two sentences, and he took it from there. What sounds more likable to you? Version one:

> *Ned:* Hold on a second, Allen. I'm just finishing an article on roller coasters.
> *Allen:* Roller coasters? Whatever got you interested in that?

Or version two:

> *Ned:* Hold on a second, Allen. I'm just finishing an article on roller coasters.
> *Allen:* That's so interesting. I just read about how Sandusky, Ohio, had a big roller coaster.

You know, the roller coaster guy probably thinks no one in his building knows about roller coasters, or figures that people would think him childish for having such an interest in them.

A few years ago I lost a potential client because I ignored my own rule. I started a conversation on a topic about which I wasn't three paragraphs deep. I also started with a bad question. In the law, you often hear that an attorney shouldn't ask the witness a question unless the attorney knows the answer. It applies here.

I was introduced to a senior executive in retail and was asked to join him for lunch. We met in his office with the intention of walking to the restaurant. On one wall was displayed a picture of a horse and rider jumping a barrier. I should've looked at it and said, "I read somewhere that the horses in these events have to be eight years old or older." Or I could've said, "In the Olympic events, I think I read that there are something like eleven or twelve obstacles." He would've loved that. He would've relished the chance to talk about something he loved, and he would've found me likable as a result. Instead I said, "Is that your wife?" He looked startled and replied, "No. That's me." Good-bye client. Good-bye retail that year.

Use Full-On Flattery

I am only going to say this about "big F" Flattery: most of the time it works. Can you find anything wrong with these statements?

"Great idea. Let's try it."

"You've lost weight. You look great."

"Nice car. Can I look inside?"

"I like your watch. Antique?"

"Nice work. Terrific effort."

"She's a great kid. How did you do it?"

"You said just the right thing."

I asked, "Can you find anything wrong with these statements?" Maybe you would respond, "A person has to be sincere when he or she says such things." My answer to that goes something like this: I hope people mean it when they are complimentary, but I would rather they say such things than not. There's significant psychological research evidence, by the way, suggesting that those who first "say it" will be the ones to ultimately "mean it." In other words, first do it and then we'll worry about the underlying feeling.

In seminars I love to pose a hypothetical. Suppose a couple, married twenty years, goes to marriage counseling because they have communication problems. The wife, in the presence of the counselor, says, "My husband rarely, if ever, says, 'I love you, sweetheart.' "

The counselor asks, "Is that true?"

The husband replies, "Well, yes. I mean we've been married all these years. She must know I love her. It's not my style to say it all the time."

The counselor says, "What do you mean, 'all the time'? She's asking you to say it *some* of the time. She loves to hear the words. It's a confirmation of the feeling you have."

The husband says, "Well, OK. I'll say it. 'Sweetie. I love ya.' How's that?" The wife's shoulders drop. She looks at the floor.

"Nope," says the counselor. "You've got to say it with feeling. Say it slowly."

The husband says, "All right. Let me do it again. "Baby. Look at me. I . . . love . . . you . . . so . . . much. I'm so sorry I've been making this sound so trivial. You . . . are . . . absolutely right." His wife looks up and smiles. The husband says, "You know, you're right. It feels good to say it."

Compliments: first say them, then feel them.

Looking Likable

I'll always remember my parents, native Yiddish speakers, using this expression to describe a sourpuss: "He has such a *farbisseneh* [embittered] expression on his face. He always looks so mean." Your face is the window into your friendly nature. If a colleague says of you, "He's such an open person," it was no doubt your face, your open, friendly face that gave your colleague that "vibe."

In our firm we've shied away from encouraging smiling as the key to a better facial expression. A smile is difficult to conjure in the absence of something that really makes you happy. Look at your pictures taken at a family gathering when the photographer said, "Smile now. Happy happy. Say cheese." Most of us do not like those pictures. The better selections in your album were taken when you weren't looking, right?

Your eyes and the entire upper part of your face, however, can be consciously made to look friendlier. If you lift your eyebrows up or squint a bit, you will look much friendlier. You won't have that *farbisseneh* look on your face.

Remember, you are judged for your behavior while talking and while listening. Even if your manner while talking is less openly friendly, your listening or reacting manner can more than make up for it. If you have a pleasant facial expression and seem to be "cheering" the talker on, she'll appreciate it. As I mentioned in Chapter Six, research has found that people who listen with their mouth slightly open will come across as more open to the speaker's ideas than those who listen with their mouth closed.

Treading Water

Recently I talked with a manager in pharmaceuticals. He's been with the company for eleven years. We were sitting at lunch when he laid out some interesting thinking. He had been mulling about the right coaching topics for people at his level—for people with a little more tenure than newcomers—and for people in senior-level positions. He's a product manager, not a training specialist, but his opinion made a lot of intuitive sense. He's recommending interpersonal skills coaching for people in senior positions lest they forget how important being open and friendly is as you become more senior in an organization.

He drew a picture of a watertank. The bottom part of the tank represented the skills one needs at the start. He felt that people at this level should receive not only technical training but also training in team cooperation and interpersonal communication. He said that as a part of learning to network, people need to know how important it is to be likable, easy to get along with, and easy to work with. He said, "People need to learn to argue, debate, and negotiate in a way that doesn't leave hard feelings."

He felt that in your first supervisory roles, you need to learn how to delegate and how to demonstrate the trust that comes with delegating, and to continue to study how senior management wants things done.

He said that senior executives put so much emphasis on strategic thinking and on the importance of getting to the point that they have to "tread water" to remember how to be team players or simply to be nice to subordinates. By treading water, he meant that if they didn't work at it, they would sink. In other words, he felt that a lot of senior executives had to constantly remind themselves to be likable, friendly, and open.

8

SO SMART, BUT LACKS ENERGY AND PASSION AND DRIVE

Several years ago, I spoke to a group of twenty women. Assertive Behavior for Women was a popular title in the 1980s and into the 1990s. I have to say that our firm didn't subscribe to, and still does not subscribe to, the whole notion of separate skills for women . . . but I digress.

One of the women said, "I know I come across to many people as a wallflower. People say I don't do anything to get myself noticed. I guess I am a quiet and reserved person. What can I do about that?" What a wonderful way to end a question: "What can I do about that?"

Before I could even clear my throat, one of her coworkers said, "If this is a safe harbor, if this is a place where we can coach each other without worrying about its being an insult, I'll offer this: you don't wear any makeup or lipstick. Makeup draws others' attention to us. It's an easy way to seem more outgoing." I looked at the first woman and nodded as if to say, "She's right. She's absolutely right. And you owe her a thank you."

Instead of a thank you, the woman said, "Well, that's just not *me*." And I said, "Well duh. Of course it's not you. That's why you came to the seminar. You came, I think, to learn how to do some things that don't come naturally. Did you come here to hear me say, 'Anything goes' or 'Just be yourself'"? I continued. "Here you have a person who takes a gamble because she cares about you, and you simply say, 'That's not me.'

"Believe me," I said, "if I could sell a cosmetic product, a tube of lipstick for ten bucks, that will make a person look a little more extroverted . . . like they were 'reaching out' to others . . . I'd do it in a heartbeat."

Showing Passion for Your Work

As much as I have loved writing about competence, composure, character, and likability, I must admit that my pet interest over the years has been this final one: extroversion, or what we've come to call *high energy*. So many people have been labeled, fairly or unfairly, with these kinds of statements:

"So smart, but so reserved and quiet"

"So smart, but so slow to deliver"

"So smart, but so very introverted"

"So smart, but so monotone"

"So smart, but so timid"

"So smart, but so hard to connect with"

Any consultancy involved in coaching people about credibility could make a fine living with no other area to serve but this one peculiar issue. In fact, in 99 percent of the world's seminars on public speaking, a participant with a monotone is called out for needing improvement more than anyone else. Well, those seminars always remind people to "gesture more," so maybe gesturing is a close second.

Anyway, in Chapter Seven I briefly referred to the Myers-Briggs Type Indicator (MBTI). In the context of communicating a more sociable, likable demeanor, I mentioned the extroverted facet of the MBTI.

I want to return to this issue. The Myers-Briggs experts, the facilitators who bring this message to the corporate world, are very, very careful to explain that one should *not* draw qualitative conclusions from the results of the test. They say things like, "Please, please, please do not think that it is 'better' to be extroverted than introverted. It is simply indicating your preference. When your colleagues know your preference, it improves communication." Sorry, folks, but this is a canard, a myth, and a bogus conclusion.

A few years ago an unmarried female colleague at CDA accompanied me to a client's three-day off-site to work with me on delivering a credibility seminar. The term *off-site* describes a corporate meeting held someplace other than the company's headquarters. The client had arranged for participants to go through the MBTI testing and a facilitated debriefing prior to getting started with the two of us. We sat in on the MBTI portion in the morning. We were to begin after lunch.

The facilitator asked the larger group to break up into smaller groups. Their task was to come up with synonyms for the word *extroverted* and synonyms for the word *introverted*. Here is a reasonable facsimile of the group's list:

Extroverted	*Introverted*
Outgoing	Shy
Loud	Quiet
Likes a good party	Reserved
Arrogant	Analytical
Energetic	Monotone
Animated	Likes to be alone

I whispered to my colleague, "Victoria, if you had a choice in being set up for a blind date, which would you choose: Mr. Extroverted, with a description matching the one here, or Mr. Introverted, with his description?" She said, "Even though I'm a little introverted myself, I'd go with Mr. Extroverted." She smiled and said, "I'd be taking a risk on the 'arrogant' piece, but the date would probably be more fun than one with Mr. Introverted."

By and large, people who watch you, evaluate you, judge you, and determine your value to the organization like to see you display a certain amount of energy. You can demonstrate that energy in so many ways. You might

- Come to work early
- Stay late
- Talk loud
- Walk fast
- Push people to work faster

- Volunteer for assignments
- Work a room

The possibilities are endless. But rest assured, your colleagues and most certainly your "seniors" like to see you with "a passion for the job," "a fire in your belly." Sometimes a client will say, "I don't know why coming to work earlier makes such a difference around here. A lot of the people who do simply read the *Wall Street Journal* until 8:30 A.M. or so." The folks at the *WSJ* would argue that reading their paper is a terrific use of time. But more important, no one looks at exactly what we're doing when we come in early. No one cares that we do it to beat the traffic. It simply says, "I like to get started early." It shows passion for work. And staying later to make up for coming in late doesn't help that much.

I've been telling this story to seminar participants for years. With apologies to my son, Matt, it goes like this:

When Matt played Little League baseball, he was not his coach's dream player. He never missed a game, but he didn't, shall we say, play with an inner fire. His mom and I joked that when all the other parents would scream, "Down and ready Rockies," they were looking at Matt lazing about in the outfield.

At one particular turn at bat, Matt took four poor pitches and drew a walk. He laid his bat in the dirt and calmly walked to first base. Some of the team parents were yelling at him as he strode toward the base: "You're doggin' it, Matt. Hustle, hustle, hustle."

When the game was over and we all got in the car for the drive home, Matt expressed his philosophy of baseball: "Dad, if I want to walk to first base when I draw a walk, I don't see why anyone should care. [Pete Rose, I hope you are not reading this.] I earned it. I'll just take my time."

I dutifully explained to Matt that baseball fans love to see a kid with a lot of passion and energy "for the game." In fact, I tried to give him a life lesson about showing energy in life in general. I probably said, "People will always want to see you run to first base, so to speak." No doubt he said, "Dad, save it for your clients."

In *Human Communication* (Burgoon, Hunsaker, & Dawson, 1994, p. 45), the authors write that "the outgoing person who engages readily in communication situations is considered to be an extrovert." I add to that, *whether they truly are or are not*. A person who talks, who is not timid, is often called a dynamic person. Every client whom others experience as "low key," and whom I've encouraged to get a little more "high key" says, "But can't a person go a little overboard? I don't want to be a 'cheerleader' type and I'd be phony if I did." Well, the answer is "yes." Yes, any *one* can do any *thing* too much. Some listeners refer to people who go overboard as overcarbonated or overcaffeinated. In Chapter Eleven I'll be talking about the pitfalls of going overboard. I warn against becoming "overcarbonated." But let me say this: for every one client who has been asked to "tone it down," I've had nine clients for whom others have suggested they "crank it up."

Burgoon, Hunsaker, and Dawson (1994, p. 46) note further that "A person who is too introverted may make communication so tedious and effortful that we simply give up." It's hard work to communicate with a person who has little to say. We like people who can strike a balance . . . between being the life of the party and a crashing bore. Extroverted people, people who show this quality whether truly possessed of it or not, hold others' attention and are generally perceived as more interesting.

Looking Excited

My dad learned English by watching evangelists on Sunday morning. Well, he probably had a few different strategies for learning English, but televised religion was one of them. And West Virginia was a hotbed for some of the most talented preachers on television. Our rabbi was a talented speaker himself and a model of gravitas. But Rex Humbard, Ernst Angley, and Oral Roberts came on before *Meet the Press*. Sometimes I wonder if they had something to do with my interest in communication. Dad thought that the preachers pronounced each word distinctly and walked on stage like "they know where they're going." He said he used some of the techniques when working on his sales floor. For instance, if Rex Humbard on Sunday said, "Feel the power of the anointing," my dad on Monday would say to a customer, "Feel the power of good wool."

I'm not surprised that evangelical Christians love going to church, because the service is so animated. It's a production. There's sophisticated lighting, and it's very loud. People dance, and the stage has wind tunnels that blow sheets to create special effects. There are spotlights on the singers. There are sometimes big screens that project images of happy people doing fun things. The people in the pews often sing and dance and laugh and yell. It's a testament to projecting faith in an exuberant way. People like to see and often be a part of a high-energy experience. One of my friends in Charleston, West Virginia, told me that the downtown churches, the traditional churches that used to have two services on Sunday morning, are losing some younger, former parishioners to the evangelical churches outside town. Younger people want a higher-energy experience, and thousands of people are showing up for church.

Why Your Hands Matter

"I'm Italian—we use our hands." The way you gesture, the way you move your body in general, has a way of making you appear bigger—or smaller. I've often compared a person in a room to a ship in the ocean. The bigger the ship, the more water it displaces. Your body, in a way, displaces air in a room. The more it displaces, the more excited you look. I'm not talking about body size—after all, a huge body displaces a lot of air. I'm talking about the way your arms move away from your body. If someone says about you, "He really filled the room with excitement," that person's perception has some real physicality about it. My clients who naturally move their hands sometimes attribute it to their Italian heritage. Whether Italian or Serbian, Norwegian or Bolivian, hands signal a higher level of passion about your message.

9

SO SMART, BUT HAS IT OUT FOR SOME PEOPLE

How Management Styles Can Cause Compliance Issues

With Lloyd Loomis, Esq., Lewis, Brisbois, Bisgaard and Smith

"Charlie is unbelievably talented *and* has been around here longer than anyone else so he knows our system, *and he's a wonderful individual contributor, and* it would be tragic to lose him, but . . . we're going to have to let him go. He intimidates many of his subordinates, and now two of them are bringing a lawsuit alleging a 'hostile work environment.'"

The HR managers, directors, vice presidents, and senior vice presidents who tell me things like this are always so melancholy in the telling. They start with a sigh and end with an angry grunt.

This sort of call marks the start of a coaching engagement. We get these calls because a supervisor, manager, or senior executive has shown an intimidating and harassing personal style toward somebody else.

At First, It Seems So Minor

Recently one patron said, "Allen, the problems *start* with the 'smallest' offenses." By emphasizing "smallest," the caller meant offenses that could look or sound innocent on paper and usually don't involve hostile language like cursing. Those small offenses continue without management intervention. For instance, the employee won't be invited to a meeting or won't be included in a group lunch. Maybe he or she won't be told about a job opportunity. Maybe the employee will turn in some assigned work and not get an acknowledgment. Some people use the term *micro-etiquette*. They point out examples of micro-etiquette errors: the behavior of someone who will not turn his entire body to speak to a subordinate, but only turns his head in the other's direction, and maybe not even that! The employee may say that he or she took that as a sign of being less deserving than a more favored employee.

I just completed a seminar back East. I began the day by observing a "real-time" meeting with the manager and his subordinates. The manager had invited his boss to the meeting to brief everyone about changes the company was making in their approach to selling a product. The manager's boss, Dick, did a sterling job on the briefing. He was terrific, and I took the time to tell him so. When the bosses' boss attends a meeting with subordinates, the meeting takes on a different tone. Everyone wants a little "face time" or exposure with this "honored guest." The littlest nod of agreement from this person can make a subordinate's day. At the same time, even mild disapproval or, worse, a comment being ignored, can ruin someone's day. And it's exacerbated when it happens in front of the whole team. One of the subordinates took the risk of disagreeing with Dick. She turned toward him, had eye contact, expressed a clear message, and said her piece with the proper tone of voice. Well, he didn't give her the time of day. He didn't turn toward her. He didn't look at her. He didn't respond to her. He made the facial expression that says, "I don't know where you're going with that." I asked her later if she noticed it, and she said, "Yes. And so did everyone else. I felt this big." She put her thumb and index finger together. Dick didn't realize his mistake. These things are almost always unintentional.

According to the typical HR executive description, situations degenerate from benign to malignant. For example, at first the employee is on the receiving end of a yelling fit. After dishing out a few of those without a formal complaint, the perpetrator seemingly gets comfortable with this level of bad behavior.

Eventually, the offender will scream, rant, and perhaps throw something against the wall. These emotional and very intense moments are hard to substantiate, but when they happen, the victim says, "That's it! I've had it." The victim's next stop is either HR or a labor attorney or both.

Here's a recent case. If you want to look it up, the full name is *Equal Employment Opportunity Commission, Plaintiff, and Carol Christopher; Julie Bhend; Carmela Chamara, Plaintiffs-Intervenors-Appellants* v. *National Education Association, Alaska; National Education Association, Plaintiff-Appellant, and Carol Christopher; Julie Bhend; Carmela Chamara, Plaintiffs-Intervenors* v. *National Education Association, Alaska; National Education Assocation, Defendants-Appellees.* It's a terrific example of a case of a hostile work environment that does not involve sexual harassment. The entire story is one of communication behavior run amok.

According to the facts, NEA-Alaska is a labor union that represents teachers and other public employees. NEA-Alaska made Thomas Harvey an executive director in 1998, and he began working in Anchorage. Carol Christopher was an employee there. Julie Bhend and Carmela Chamara were part of the support staff. Christopher resigned in February of 2000. Chamara resigned in August of 2000. They testified that they resigned because of Harvey's conduct.

The record reveals numerous episodes of Harvey's shouting in a loud and hostile manner at female employees. The shouting was frequent, profane, and often public.

Harvey's verbal conduct also had a hostile physical component. Christopher said Harvey regularly came up behind her silently as she was working, stood over her, and watched her for no apparent reason. The relevant content of the behavior included shouting, screaming, foul language, and invading personal space.

Goodwill: Your Boss Wants You to Succeed

In Chapter One, I described the five categories of credibility and briefly introduced you to the latest research on a sixth, *goodwill*. It's this category of personal credibility, goodwill, that explains an employee's first feelings of discontent and, ultimately, the decision to file a formal complaint.

This quotation refers to research conducted with students and teachers (McCroskey and Teven, 1999), but it is also relevant to relations between a supervisor and a subordinate.

> We certainly are going to listen more attentively to a person who we believe has our best interests at heart than to one who we think might be wanting to put one over on us. But the caring construct does not suggest the opposite of caring is malicious intent. It is just indifference. Thus it is not likely the student will automatically reject what the teacher says if he or she is treated like a number. Rather, such treatment is just as likely to make the student more suspicious of the teacher's motives. Teachers do not have to be devoted to their students in order for the students to learn. But if the teacher engages in behaviors that communicate such positive intent to the student, it is likely the student will engage in more effort to learn what the teacher is trying to teach.

So, an employee who feels that her boss has her best interests at heart will work better than one who does not have that feeling. And, in fact, an employee who feels that she is being "treated like a number" will do just fine too. In our world, problems begin when an employee feels the true opposite of caring: malicious intent, or "badwill."

I referred to the term *goodwill* in my introduction. *Goodwill* breaks down into three aspects: understanding, empathy, and responsiveness. If someone shows *understanding*, we have the feeling that she knows our ideas, feelings, and needs. She seems to know when our feelings are hurt, when we have a problem or need her help. If we know someone understands our worries, we feel close to her because she seems to care about us. In the case of understanding, if someone shows badwill, she understands that we're worried and makes it worse. Badwill means that someone knows our ideas and needs but denigrates them in order to make us feel useless.

Empathy is a person's ability to identify with another's feelings. That person would not only understand the other's views but would accept those views as valid. When someone shows another empathy, he comes across as caring about the other person. In the NEA case, for example, Christopher had told Harvey she wanted to spend a day taking care of her dying sister. She asked for the Labor Day weekend as legitimate days off, but then took an extra day. When she returned, Harvey asked her how her sister was. When she replied, "Not very good," and "Should I bring anything to the meeting this morning?" Harvey got angry and yelled at her. Christopher testified, "He knows my sister is dying. He knows how heavy my heart is, and he can say that?" What a perfect example of a lack of empathy.

Responsiveness describes a person's acknowledgment of another person's attempts to communicate. It's a measure of how quickly someone reacts to another's communication. It shows attentiveness and the appearance of listening. People who are responsive come across as caring.

Harvey's employees might not have chosen to sue had he shown understanding and empathy. There might not have been a legal action if he had been neutral, but instead he went entirely in the wrong direction and demonstrated that his needs came first.

If you are an HR professional, you would be wise to offer internal seminars or coaching (or both) for employees, long before the need arises, on understanding, empathy, and responsiveness.

A Labor Lawyer's Perspective (Lloyd Loomis)

Managing people is a very difficult job at best. The total array of management tools and approaches to making management decisions is limited by various policies, procedures, and expectations of the institution in which a manager operates. Since the late 1950s, numerous federal and state laws have been passed to prohibit various forms of discrimination. Also, new laws have provided employees with numerous other rights in terms of time off from work with protected reinstatement.

Violation of these laws and the resulting litigation not only result in liability for the employer but in certain circumstances can result in personal liability for the manager. In the famous Baker McKenzie sex harassment case, the jury entered a verdict against the individual defendant for several hundred thousand dollars.

Almost everyone is covered by some kind of discrimination law. Just when we think that there can't be another category that needs protection from discrimination, a new one is created. (I do believe the California legislature is the most creative in this regard.)

Here's a quick list of the protected categories:

Age
Race
Gender
Disability—mental and physical
Color
Religion
National origin
Marital status
Sexual orientation
Veteran status
Medical condition
Being a person who has recovered from cancer
Transgender

Harassment on the basis of any of these categories is prohibited.

And, of course, if a person makes any kind of a charge or claim of discrimination, he or she is protected from retaliation. Legal proceedings involving claims of discrimination, harassment, and retaliation are extremely time consuming, they interfere with business operations, and they are expensive. If your case goes to trial in a metropolitan area, you're looking at hundreds of thousands of dollars.

One of the most significant aspects of these cases is that they are tried before a jury, a group of six to twelve people from all walks of life and with various views and experiences. Juries are unpredictable! This group of people coming in unfamiliar with the facts will ultimately determine whether a company and its supervisors and managers have discriminated against an employee or a group of employees.

What is discrimination? It is very hard to define. Generally, *discriminating* means making a decision based on some characteristic that favors some and disadvantages others. But not all discrimination is unlawful or immoral—making a decision about the color of shoes that you wear or making a decision to choose a particular employee for a promotion because of his or her past job performance is discrimination, but not prohibited discrimination.

It *is* prohibited discrimination when the decision to promote a certain employee is based on the race of the employee as compared to the race of the other employee under consideration, or when race is a prominent or motivating factor.

The law doesn't require that persons bringing discrimination claims show or prove a specific intent to discriminate; cases can be won on the basis of circumstantial evidence. This kind of evidence usually involves a pattern of conduct that may suggest discrimination or inconsistent treatment. (Of course, there may be true evidence of discrimination, harassment, or retaliation. Managers who exhibit this behavior need either to be removed from their positions or to undergo significant behavior modifications.)

The point is that subjective perceptions as to what is inconsistent treatment or a pattern of conduct suggesting discrimination will often trigger a lawsuit or a claim and may also cause a jury to find discrimination or wrongful conduct by an employer or supervisor even when the real truth of the matter is that no illegal or wrongful conduct was present.

In other words, many employment discrimination claims are not really the result of actual discrimination, but rather discrimination as perceived by the employee. The supervisor or manager may have very sound business-related, nondiscriminatory reasons for taking an employment action, such as a promotion, transfer, demotion, or termination. But the employee affected by such an action will view these situations in terms of his or her interpretation of the communication from the supervisor and the context of that communication. Supervisors should not forget that coworkers will also "help" the affected employee interpret the communication.

Because of the crucial role of perception and interpretation of behavior, obviously credibility and communication style play a very large part in workplace disputes and litigation. Supervisors and managers need to realize that they are in effect on duty 24/7— employees are watching and listening to everything.

Poor style and bad communication are the culprits for a large percentage of the cases brought to court. A critical part of a manager's style must be to treat people consistently; exceptions cause problems. Playing favorites breeds resentment and may ultimately lead to litigation. Managers who believe they are smart and cute and able to get away with anything are waiting for disaster. And of course the issue of respect is also critical.

The following cases illustrate how poor communication style, lack of credibility, and lack of empathy and respect often lead to litigation.

The recent decision of the California Supreme Court in *Yanowitz* v. *L'Oreal U.S.A.* (August 11, 2005) is a clear example of how a manager's style and perception of what was appropriate can be completely off base.

If you pick up any fashion or women's magazine, you know that L'Oreal is a very prominent name in cosmetics and high fashion. Its models are young and beautiful. Ms. Yanowitz was a regional sales manager for Northern California and the Pacific Northwest. She held this job from 1986 until 1998, when she left the company. Yanowitz was recognized as a very successful manager by the employer in 1996 and 1997. She received high bonus payments and other forms of recognition.

However, the story doesn't end there. In fall 1997, the plaintiff and her supervisor toured various stores in the San Francisco Bay Area to see how a new marketing campaign was being carried out.

After the tour of one particular store in San Jose, the supervisor told Yanowitz to terminate the employment of a dark-skinned female sales associate because he did not find the woman to be sufficiently physically attractive. The supervisor expressed a preference for fair-skinned blondes. The supervisor told the plaintiff, "Get me somebody hot."

The plaintiff did not terminate the sales associate. There was a second tour of the San Jose store, and again the supervisor told the plaintiff to terminate the sales associate and again reiterated his preference for fair-skinned blondes.

What a message to Ms. Yanowitz! Nevertheless, she did not terminate the sales associate in question. It so happened that the sales associate was one of the top sellers of L'Oreal products in the Macy's West chain.

Ms. Yanowitz did not make any complaints about being told to terminate the sales associate because of her appearance. But the record reflects that she believed that it could have been a violation of the California Fair Employment and Housing Act (FEHA) to terminate the sales associate because of her physical appearance. Each time she was asked about terminating the sales associate, she would ask her supervisor to give her a basis for the termination.

But the supervisor could not leave well enough alone. He went out and solicited negative information about Ms. Yanowitz, and his campaign against Ms. Yanowitz commenced. She was criticized for her management style and for being too aggressive.

At one point, there was a complaint about a sales promotion in Ms. Yanowitz's area, and the supervisor screamed at Ms. Yanowitz, "I'm sick and tired of all the fuck-ups." Further, memos were written criticizing Ms. Yanowitz's performance. Ultimately, Ms. Yanowitz went on disability and was replaced by another employee.

Then she sued. Her complaint set forth various causes of action including a claim for retaliation.

The plaintiff claimed that she refused to fire the sales associate because she believed that such termination would be a violation of

California FEHA and that this refusal to terminate the sales associate was "protected activity" under the Act. She further claimed that all the negative criticism, yelling, and so on was retaliation for her engaging in protected activity and was a campaign to develop pretextual grounds to terminate her. Thus her leaving was a constructive discharge. By that term we mean that an employer allows intolerable working conditions to continue, that the employer knew and didn't take any action to rectify those, and that a reasonable person wouldn't work under those conditions.

The California Supreme Court first found that "protected activity" does include the opposition to conduct that the employee reasonably and in good faith believes to be discriminatory, even if such conduct is later found not to be a violation of FEHA.

The court noted that the order to terminate the sales associate was not based on sales or work performance and further that there was no general policy as to physical appearance for men or women sales associates. The court had no problem deciding that under these circumstances, the termination of the sales associate could have violated the California discrimination laws.

The real question was whether Yanowitz's failure to complain to L'Oreal about the termination order would defeat her claim. L'Oreal claimed that because Yanowitz never told anyone about her fear that terminating the sales associate would violate FEHA, the company could not have been retaliating against her for her belief.

Yanowitz argued that in response to the order, she requested the supervisor to provide "adequate justification" for the termination, and there was no response from the supervisor. Yanowitz claimed that these exchanges were sufficient to put her supervisor on notice that she felt that it would violate the law to terminate the sales associate under these circumstances.

The court agreed and stated, "We agree with Yanowitz that when the circumstances surrounding an employee's conduct are sufficient to establish that an employer knew that an employee's refusal to comply with an order was based on the employee's reasonable belief that the order is discriminatory, an employer may not avoid the reach of the

FEHA's anti-retaliation provision by relying on the circumstance that the employee did not explicitly inform the employer that she believed the order was discriminatory."

What an example of poor style, lack of listening, and management irresponsibility causing significant harm to the employer both financially and otherwise. Don't forget that every employee at L'Oreal knows what happened and what a fool the manager had been, and unfortunately for L'Oreal, the communication to employees was very clear and very negative.

It should also be noted that there may have been some business justification for the criticism of Yanowitz, but the possible existence of deficient job performance was completely eclipsed by the ignorant behavior of this supervisor.

In today's work environment, everyone must consider the need for both objective and subjective compliance with these very important and difficult standards prohibiting discrimination.

Maybe L'Oreal had a point about not being put on notice about Yanowitz's belief that the order violated the law, but the supervisor's lack of class and integrity and his negative communication about the worth of people was just too prominent.

Another recent case that demonstrates how a manager's style, lack of respect, and character can lead to disaster is *Miller* v. *Department of Corrections* (California Supreme Court, July 18, 2005).

This case involves claims by two female employees of the California prison system that the warden provided favorable treatment to several female employees with whom he was having sexual affairs and that this created a hostile work environment—in other words, sexual harassment.

The general rule from a legal standpoint is that the fact that a male supervisor provides isolated favorable treatment to a female employee with whom the supervisor is having a consensual affair does not constitute sexual harassment. (It does, of course, send a terrible message to the other employees.) However, in this case, the affairs were numerous and the favoritism widespread, and the court found that the effect on other women employees may have created a hostile work environment and therefore violated the discrimination law.

The facts in the case are somewhat extreme. The warden was having affairs with at least three female employees. He ordered subordinates to award a promotion to an unqualified woman. One of the women bragged to other women about using the affair with the warden to gain favorable treatment. Favorable work assignments and special privileges were granted. The court record reflected evidence that coworkers who observed what was going on "were saying things like, 'what do I have to do, fuck my way to the top?'" The court had no problem finding that these allegations did support a claim for sexual harassment. In coming to this conclusion, the court stated that "when such sexual favoritism in a workplace is sufficiently widespread it may create an unlawful hostile work environment in which the demeaning message is conveyed to female employees that they are viewed by management as 'sexual playthings' or that the way required for women to get ahead in the workplace is by engaging in sexual conduct with their supervisor or the management."

Now, while this fact pattern is extreme, the observation of the court as to how employees view the situation is accurate and applies even in cases where the situation involves the supervisor's having an affair with only one female employee.

Favoritism gives a very strong negative message to employees. It undermines almost every aspect of the relationship between the supervisor and employees. The supervisor loses credibility and in a short period of time will become very ineffective.

Employees' perception of favoritism can take many forms, and supervisors need to be aware of this. The following recent case is an example.

In this case, part of a female employee's allegations for constructive discharge was that on two occasions her supervisor, along with several of her male coworkers, went to a strip club immediately after the conclusion of a company-sponsored event. Of course she was not invited, and she would not have gone even if she had been. But her claim was that she had been precluded from time with her boss, that he was showing favoritism toward male employees, and that she was being disadvantaged in her career.

Although there is no hard evidence that the plaintiff was actually disadvantaged in any way, she firmly believed what she was saying, and as a result of these events and other claims of favoritism, she quit her job and sued the company for sex discrimination. It was clear that the supervisor was totally oblivious to what he was doing and to the message he was sending to his employees. It is not hard to understand the feelings of disrespect and anger created by this supervisor's lack of empathy for his employee.

This case is yet another reminder that what supervisors and management say or do sends messages to employees all the time.

Lack of respect is a very powerful message, and a supervisor's failure to understand what is required in order to show a proper level of respect can create problems and legal difficulty.

The case of *Mamdouh El-Hahkem* v. *BJY Inc.* out of the U.S. Court of Appeals for the Ninth Circuit (2005) is a prime example.

In this case, the plaintiff brought a claim of racial discrimination against his employer and the CEO personally. The racial discrimination claim stemmed from the CEO's repeatedly calling the plaintiff "Manny" despite the plaintiff's objections. At one point, the plaintiff suggested that if the CEO had problems pronouncing the plaintiff's first name (Mamdouh), the CEO should call the plaintiff by his last name, El-Hakem. The CEO responded with the suggestion that the plaintiff be called "Hank." Needless to say, this was not accepted by the plaintiff. He quit and filed suit for constructive discharge.

The jury held that the CEO's insistence on using a westernized name for the plaintiff rather than his Arabic name constituted racial discrimination and awarded the plaintiff damages. The Court of Appeals affirmed the award of the jury. The court concluded that: "A group's ethnic characteristics encompass more than its member's skin color and physical traits. Names are often a proxy for race and ethnicity."

The court found that the CEO's refusal to use the plaintiff's actual name constituted racial discrimination in violation of the law.

It appears that the CEO simply had no respect for his employee as a person and clearly communicated this disrespect to the plaintiff. The plaintiff apparently was proud of his heritage, and the CEO's refusal to acknowledge this caused the plaintiff to file a lawsuit and the company to lose an employee and spend a significant amount of money in legal fees and damages. Empathy and respect could have easily avoided this entire matter.

10

ASSESSING YOUR OWN CREDIBILITY

www.essessnet.com

It should be pretty easy to assess your current level of credibility, but so many people tell me that they don't get a lot of really substantial advice or insights from their boss or peers in their annual performance review. If your company hasn't made a 360° type of assessment available to you, you can use ours for free for a full year. We call it www.essessnet.com. The results of this set of questions will put you on the road to an admirable credibility reputation. You'll be able to get a quantitative reading of your current level of credibility as well as have access to reference articles and books.

CDA's Flagship Question Set

Here are the firm's original twelve questions; we've asked them continually for nearly thirty years. You'll be asking your colleagues

1. Do I communicate in a clear and concise manner?
2. When you are talking, do I appear to be listening?
3. Do I come across as having a broad, strategic view of the business?
4. Do I come across as upbeat and friendly?
5. Would you describe me as decisive, someone who pushes forward and moves things along?
6. Do I treat you as an equal as opposed to having a condescending quality?

7. Do I strike you as being open-minded?

8. When I am asked a question, do I get to the point as opposed to giving you a long-winded, complex answer?

9. Do I handle stress well and come across as composed in high-pressure situations?

10. Do I invite or at least accept constructive criticism as opposed to sounding defensive?

11. Do I come across as value-added on topics for which I am supposed to have expertise?

12. Do I come across as a problem solver and create a problem-solving environment?

If you think again about the five credibility factors, you will see that the questions were intended to reflect or address those factors. Here are the five factors with some of the corresponding questions:

1. Competence

    Do I come across as having a broad, strategic view of the business?

2. Composure

    Do I handle stress well?

3. Character

    Do I treat you as an equal?

4. Likability (formerly sociability)

    Do I come across as upbeat and friendly?

5. High energy (formerly extroversion)

    Am I decisive, someone who pushes forward and moves things along?

Credibility Is Not One Point in Time

We've designed a computer program to enable you to receive some initial credibility ratings from any person or group you choose *and* to track your progress for a year. After all, it's unfair to gather feedback at just one point in time. The way you track your feedback should look just like the way you'd track a stock or mutual fund.

You should be able to get continuous feedback from colleagues, at least as much as you want, and see how things have changed since the last time you checked. Essessnet lets you do this. The graphical interface you'll see for your feedback on www.essessnet.com will look like Figure 10.1.

Figure 10.1 shows a hypothetical client's "feedback portfolio." Looking from left to right, you see the first seven questions of the original recipe 12; the client's current score out of a possible highest rating of 5.0; how the score has changed since the last time he looked; and links to various charts, graphs, and open-ended comments. At the light bulb icon, there are links to information on every single question.

Figure 10.1. Essessnet Results.

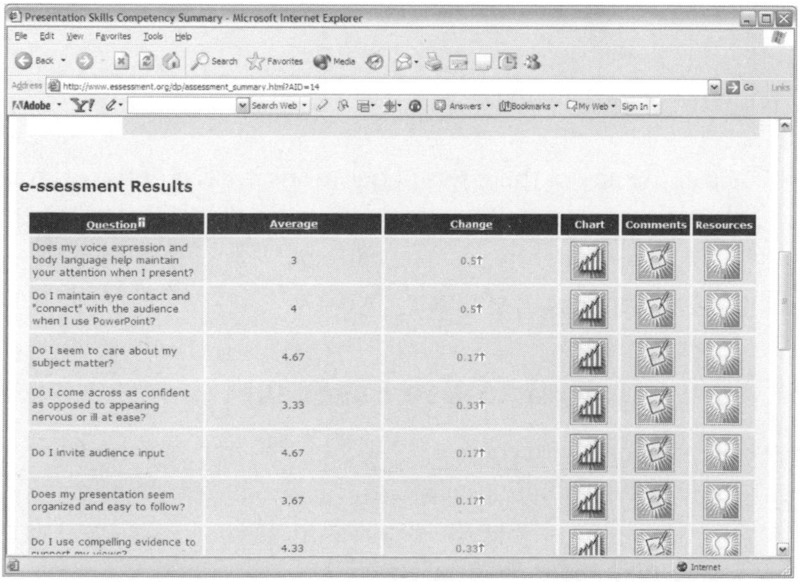

Over the years, we've expanded the original set to include seventeen additional "competencies":

1. Communication
2. Conflict management
3. Constructive criticism
4. Decision making
5. Downward communication
6. Interpersonal relationships
7. Interviewer skills
8. Interviewing skills
9. Leadership
10. Management skills
11. Presentation skills
12. Problem solving
13. Strategic thinking
14. Team communication
15. Team player
16. Technical ability
17. Upward communication

You can use any of these sets of questions instead of the original credibility questionnaire if you so desire. I've included all of the questions sets in Appendix A. You can read through them to see if they make more sense in your specific case.

How to Use Essessnet

Log on to www.essessnet.com, and you'll be directed as to how to register for the questionnaire that seems the best fit for your situation. Think ahead about whose feedback you would like to solicit and write down their e-mail addresses. You'll need those to register. Choose people whose opinion of you is of most concern to you. It's not useful to skew your list toward people who think you're terrific on all counts.

Once that's done, you'll be ready to send out your request for feedback and should soon start to see some e-mails telling you that your feedback has come in. Take the scores and comments seriously. Use *So Smart, But . . .* to figure out how to address the advice you receive. In the end, people will say of you, "So smart, and very open to feedback."

In addition to the quantitative scores you'll receive, you can also view qualitative, open-ended comments. Your screen will look something like Figure 10.2.

I think it's a great convenience for a client to be able to look at feedback from any computer anywhere, at any time. I've come to call it "presidential tracking polling for all of us" because as a user you can receive solicited or unsolicited feedback all year in real time. Why should anyone wait until she's elected president to find out how she's perceived?

Figure 10.2. Open-Ended Comments.

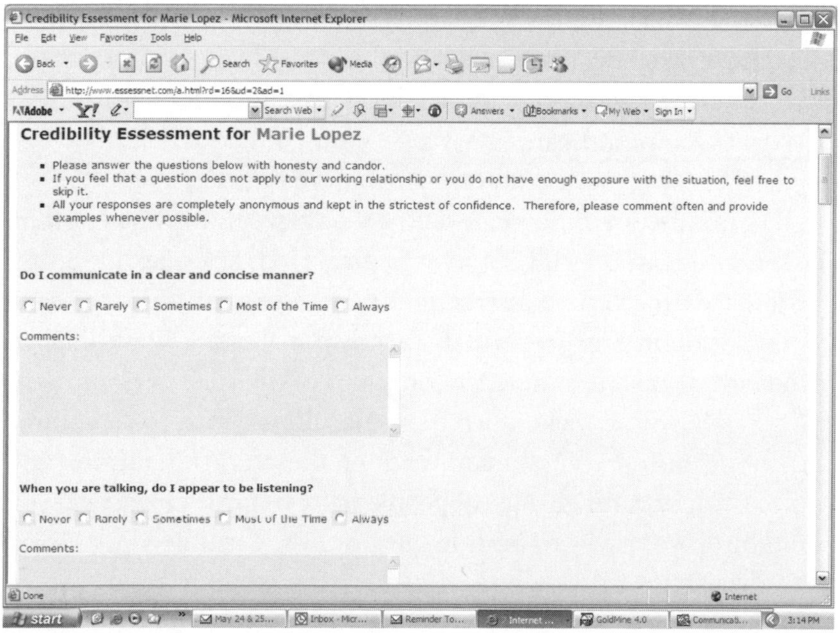

Feedback Is Not a Panacea

All feedback-gathering efforts have to be carefully thought through. One very compelling argument against 360° feedback is that no one should be focused entirely on others' perceptions. I think there is a lot of truth to that. If you take such feedback to the extreme, you would be walking too carefully through your career, afraid of stepping on a feedback land mine. For instance, if someone were to be continually reminded that his answers to questions are too detailed, he might not "let himself go," so to speak, and simply speak his mind on an important issue. A healthy attitude about feedback makes a lot of sense. After all, a leader *leads*, she doesn't only follow other people's suggestions.

One other caution: organizations should be careful not to use too many feedback-gathering processes at the same time. There have been many times in our practice when a client has said, "Allen, I'm happy to use www.essessnet.com, but I have to tell you that I'm working with a life coach [or working with a presentation skills coach or taking a seminar] where feedback is also a part of the exercise. Is that OK?" My general answer is, "Not really." I don't want a client to be "overmedicated" on feedback, as I call it. If, however, the other source uses feedback that reflects clearly different issues than the ones www.essessnet.com looks at, I'm not opposed to using more than one instrument at once.

There's also an annoyance factor that kicks in if you are asking the same person(s) to fill out a lot of 360° feedback questionnaires at the same time. These instruments take respondents a lot of time if they fill them out properly. If I were your boss, I would like to believe that you are somewhat conscious of the time commitment you are asking me to make when the feedback-gathering process starts.

But assuming you've taken care of these considerations and you've thought through a list of people you can tap for feedback, you could be on your way to finding out just how credible you are and just how much work you'll need to do to make things right.

11

SIXTEEN MIND-SETS

And Five Seminars You Shouldn't Take

As you've seen, the majority of the takeaways from *So Smart But . . .* are behavioral. You've learned to "do it this way," "say it this way," or "listen this way." In this chapter, I turn away from the behavioral focus; we're going to look at some "mind-sets," or ways of thinking about credibility, that will make your pursuit easier. (Along the way, I'll also be noting some seminars that you shouldn't bother to take.)

Before we go on, though, a word or two about the term *behavioral*. The field of study in communication studies is different from that of psychology. In psychology you can choose to study behavior, attitude, or both. Behavioral study is objective; the study of attitude is subjective. I think a communication studies student must embrace behaviorism. Communication is behavior. An attitude is not a living, breathing entity until it's expressed in words or actions.

Behavioral science deals with observable, measurable phenomena—things you can see, hear, and touch. When I tell you in Chapter Four that your ability to project your competence depends on others' hearing both the breadth and depth of your point of view, I'm stating a behavioral requirement. It is a "tip" that you can take to the bank.

Having said that, there are some conceptual notions, things every communicator ought to think about before and after he or she starts "behaving" that will have a bearing on the outcome. And here they are.

Mind-Set One: I'm Good

About a year ago, I sat with a client to help him prepare for an interview. His boss suggested that he be a candidate for a senior position in sales. He would be replacing a fellow who was retiring. Right at the start, Mike, my client, said, "No one can replace Andy. People are freaked out that he's leaving."

Mike asked me for tips on how to put together an opening statement. He asked me to work with him on answering questions. He wanted to make sure that he dressed right, sat right, and projected the appropriate level of energy. But the first thing I said was, "You don't have the right attitude going in. You're supposed to be thinking, 'I've been chomping at the bit for this job.'" I told him that his attitude could very well have an impact on his behavior.

Uh-oh. That sounds subjective. But this is an example of a mind-set.

If I tell you that you have to go into a meeting believing that you belong there, that you are absolutely necessary to a good outcome, I am encouraging you to take on an attitude. Some people call this *self-talk*. Comedian Al Franken based an entire shtick on this topic for *Saturday Night Live*. He played the character Stuart Smalley and used to say to himself, "I'm Good Enough, I'm Smart Enough, and Doggone It, People Like Me!" Some people call these "affirmations." Not that long ago, I heard Diane Sawyer interviewed. She was asked to talk about what she might do when she retired. She said, "My dad told me to do things I really like and that people need." So I tell myself and my clients, before a meeting, to think these words: "I love what I do, and they need to hear it."

One of my clients referred me to Reid Buckley, William Buckley's brother, who has a book on public speaking. Buckley tells his public speaking clients that if they let nervousness get in the way of a performance, it's a moral failure. By that he means that if you are not totally focused on giving your audience all you can give and all they deserve, then you are guilty of a moral failure. Put in self-talk

terms, you would say to yourself, "I know this topic better than anyone else. My audience deserves the best I can give. To let them
down would be to violate my morals—at least, the moral that anything worth doing is worth doing well."

Here are some things I *don't* want you to say to yourself prior to
a meeting. It's all too likely that your attitude will show in your
actions.

> I hate talking about this material, and they'll think it's a waste
> of time.
>
> These aren't my slides. I'm not ready to present them. It's just
> a dog–and-pony show.
>
> I need more time to prepare, and it's going to show.
>
> I hate pretending to be someone I'm not.

Don't forget

> "I love what I do, and they need to hear it."
>
> "No one else is as prepared to do this as I am."
>
> "I've waited for this chance, and now I've got it."

The self-talk will help you visualize a positive experience. The
visualization will help you perform better. The performance could
lead to some nice feedback. The feedback will lead right back to the
self-talk: you'll believe it all the more. As Figure 11.1 illustrates,
you'll be in a *victory* circle instead of a vicious circle.

Mind-Set Two: I've Got the Edge

I've traditionally hesitated to tell a client, "Just relax and be yourself." I haven't rebelled against the "be yourself" part, although, as
you'll soon see, I have a lot to say about that too. I don't want my
client to be artificial, because I'm afraid it would be noticed. But I'm

Figure 11.1. The Victory Circle of Positive Self-Talk.

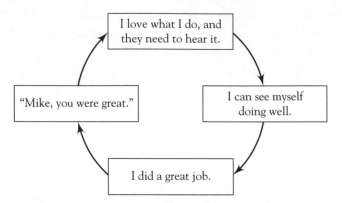

not a fan of "just relax." We have seen thousands of clients come across less credibly because they were "relaxed." When you are casual, your output will be sluggish. You'll gesture less or not at all. Your volume will drop. All the behaviors that project your natural passion will be absent.

When you interview for a job, you'll have the edge. After you get the job, you might lose it. The edge drives you to get to the interview on time. Losing it allows you to start coming in a little late. The edge drives you to prepare for a PowerPoint presentation. Losing it allows you to wing it. The edge pushes you to walk with a brisk air. Losing it allows you to shuffle.

Just as a ballplayer should take a batting stance that shows he or she means business, you should be taking a stance that shows your drive, determination, and passion.

Mind-Set Three: I'm on Top of My Game

I would run out of ink if I were to list all the clients who tell me they are so much more credible when prepared. Clients have all kinds of excuses for a less than credible day-to-day appearance:

"My boss is the real problem here."
"HR doesn't know what's what."

"No one takes meetings seriously."

"It's totally disorganized. Everything's about putting out fires."

"I've got problems at home."

It's rare when a client tells me how much more credible she was because circumstances were just right. People tend to take all the credit when things go well and to blame others, or other things, when things don't go so well. Imagine someone saying,

"The audience brought out the best me I could be."

"I only did well because I'd just heard my son got straight A's."

"My boss gets all the credit for today. She made me what I am."

Your attitude should be that you are responsible for how things could go and did go. You have to say to yourself, "I am not going to 'depend on the kindness of strangers,'" as Blanche DuBois says in *A Streetcar Named Desire*. You have to say to yourself, "No matter who is around or what can happen today, I am going to stay in control. No one is going to take me out of my game."

I facilitate hundreds of seminars every year. All of CDA's consultants do. None of us can let things get to us to such a degree that audience members would suffer for it. Every consultant has a story about "the seminar from Hell." Here is mine.

On April Fool's Day about ten years ago, I facilitated a seminar on executive credibility in downtown Los Angeles. I was working in *the* executive conference room on *the* executive-level floor. I videotaped each of eight participants as he or she spoke around the conference table. At one point I gathered all the tapes with the intention of showing them to the group.

I inserted a tape into the VCR and turned the volume down because I wanted the group to concentrate on body language. I didn't want them distracted by voice qualities. As the first tape began, I turned to the group to watch their reaction. After a minute, I saw facial expressions change from curious or intensely interested to stupefied and mortified. I turned to look at the television screen and saw *people having sex.*

Now for the "staying on top of my game" part.

I crisply turned off the VCR and said, "Let's take a break."

I played every one of those eight tapes. All of them were copies of the same porno movie, *Heat Wave.* I quickly deduced that our offices had received, not a shipment of three hundred blank VHS tapes, but a shipment of three hundred copies of *Heat Wave.*

When the participants came back into the conference room, they were not smiling. The episode might have spelled the end of a very lucrative consulting contract. It might have generated a lawsuit. But I was not going to let this take me out of my game. I told the executives about the mixed shipment. One of them said, "It was a great attention grabber." Another said, "It was so out of place, I thought at first it was an exercise tape." At lunch I purchased eight new tapes, and we ended the day all smiles.

When I say, "taken out of my game," I mean I might have overapologized, over-referred back to the incident as the day went on, lowered the level of rigor I typically bring to telling clients how I want them to improve because I would be afraid of another negative reaction, looked at them with less eye contact, and lowered my volume thinking it would make me sound softer or more gentle. In other words, I would have been a different Allen Weiner.

Mind-Set Four: They Can't Ignore Me

Another attitude that you must adopt concerns listening skills. *Absolutely no one would need listening skills if the talker had an interesting message and an interesting way to put it.*

> *"Don't Take This Seminar" Number 1: Listening Skills.* It's not the listener's job to force himself to listen. It's your job to say things listeners find interesting.

Listeners should not have to be taught to pay attention to a speaker or message that is not compelling. If ever there were a prime example of disingenuous, artificial behavior it would be that shown by a person who has been coached to feign listening.

Ten years or so ago, I got the opportunity to work with an executive leadership group at a chemical company back East. One of the group members said, "Allen, you are apparently the consultant de jour, the flavor of the month, with Hal [the CEO]. When you see him, tell him that it's not polite to go to the restroom right in the middle of our executive briefings." So I told Hal. Hal said, "You tell Rick that when he has something interesting to say and an interesting way to say it, I'll hold my water."

Recently I was talking to a school principal at one of America's largest public school districts. She shared an acronym with me: SLANT. She said she used it to show young students how to demonstrate their listening attitude, their respect, to the teacher. Here's the formula:

S—Sit up with feet on the floor.
L—Lean forward slightly.
A—Ask questions and act like you are listening.
N—Nod.
T—Track the speaker with your eyes.

I don't have a problem with students being taught how to show respect for a teacher. But if I had the choice, I'd rather teach a teacher how to teach than teach the kids how to feign listening.

If all of us have an interesting way of putting things, we'll get listeners who SLANT.

The same acronym for the teacher could be:

S—tell Stories
L—Look like you love the subject
A—Ask questions and act like you want their input
N—Nonverbally show your love of teaching
T—Take the time to prepare

Mind-Set Five: Keep It "Top Line"

As I was writing *So Smart But . . .*, I took a call from an HR director at one of America's most successful biotech companies. He said that I was going to be "hooked up" with a fellow in global operations for some executive coaching. His boss had advised the fellow that he was misreading the needs of some senior executives. "These executives see him drilling way down into detail without the ability to surface quickly. They want him to drill down on request. They'll ask the right questions, and he needs to wait for them to do so."

This call reflects an exceptionally common complaint coming from senior-level people. They want an executive summary—the breadth, so to speak, of the topic. The speaker often wants to deliver the depth, the details, and the drill-down.

All of us have to assess what listeners want and drive to it instead of giving them want *we* want—what we prepared for. Refer back to "The Thirty-Second Elevator Ride" (Chapter Two) for a formula for giving people what they need when they need it.

Mind-Set Six: We're More Alike Than Different

I have a lot to say here, and it's such a thought-provoking topic. In a nutshell, the person who's doing the judging bestows your credibility on you. If John Kerry and George W. Bush were perceived as credible candidates for the presidency, it's because voters thought it so. Why did some voters prefer Kerry? Because they believed he would act as they would act. They believed he is someone they can relate to. They believed that his causes are their causes. And, of course, the same goes for George W. Bush. We are most comfortable with people who we think are similar to us.

Think about it. We say things about each other like, "I click with him," "We have similar tastes," "We're two peas in a pod," "We share the same concerns."

In most cases, *and there are exceptions*, the person who is evaluating your credibility is likely to think more highly of you if she thinks you are like her.

I was talking about this phenomenon to a new client in Philadelphia earlier this year. He is African American, and his boss is Caucasian. My client said, "You know, Allen, you're right. [Smart guy.] My boss couldn't care less about our ethnicity. But he was annoyed recently that I came to work later than he does. He actually mentioned it. He tried to make a joke of it, but I knew he was serious."

My client was absolutely right. Similarity doesn't involve ethnicity, gender, age, sexual preference, or religion. Our studies demonstrate that similarity is judged by comparing intellect, level of energy, desire for control, friendly attitude, and the showing of respect. My client got "dinged" for coming in late because it appeared to reflect a different attitude from what his boss has with regard to when to come to work.

Everett Rogers and F. Floyd Shoemaker (1971) conducted some of the most eye-opening studies I have ever read. If ever there was a book written for academics that all of us should read, *Communication of Innovations* is that book! Here is what the authors say about the topic of similarity:

> One of the obvious principles of human communication is that the transfer of ideas occurs most frequently between a source and a receiver who are alike, similar, and homophilous. Homophily is the degree to which pairs of individuals who interact are similar in certain attributes, such as beliefs, values, education, social status, and the like. In a free-choice situation, when a source can interact with any one of a number of receivers, there is a strong tendency for him to select a receiver who is most like him [p. 14].

Notice that they don't include race, religion, age, gender, and so on. Now and then I've dropped the term "homophily" in a coaching session or seminar. It always gets the raised eyebrow. But notice: it is simply the scientific, academic term for similarity.

"Don't Take This Seminar" Number 2: Diversity Training.
Don't choose a diversity seminar over a similarity seminar. The best part of diversity seminars is the exchange of regional foods.

Mind-Set Seven: It's Not About Personality

Imagine driving on a busy stretch of interstate. You're cruising along in the fast lane doing seventy-five. Out of nowhere, a tricked-out Ford 150, jacked up eight feet off the ground, is on your tail, and the driver is blasting his horn and blinking his brights. It's as if he's screaming, "Get outta my way, you geek!"

When you get home, you will tell the story. You will attribute the actions of this driver to his personality. You'll say, "A crazy, freaked-out, doped-out jerk scared the hell out of me."

When the driver gets home he'll say, "I hope I got here on time. Is Jimmy OK?"

The people who watch us do what we do tend to attribute our actions to our personality. We tend to attribute our actions to the situation we faced when we acted. This attribution can feel entirely unfair.

If you're late for a meeting, you might say, "The traffic was horrific." Your colleague might think, "He just doesn't care about starting times." If you miss a deadline, you might say, "I didn't get the numbers from finance until this morning." Your colleague might think, "He just doesn't respect deadlines." If you are nervous during a presentation, you might say, "These weren't my slides. I just got them an hour ago." Your colleagues might think, "He's not confident when it comes to presentations."

Your credibility depends on your ability to convince your colleagues that any poor performance was shaped by the situation. In plain language, it's called getting the benefit of the doubt. If the client I mentioned earlier who has annoyed the executive committee because he's too detailed wants us to believe that he felt that a more detailed presentation was called for in "that situation," he better be able to forgo details in "the other situation." He better be truly able to adjust his performance based on the situation.

Do you know what is also so interesting? When an observer sees you doing something very impressive, he or she is less likely to attribute it to your personality than to circumstance. If you do an exceptionally good job handling yourself at a national sales meeting, the people seeing you are more likely to say, "He lucked out. He had great numbers to show" than they are to say, "He's terrific by nature." They say that sometimes. But the former is said more often. So, the mind-set message here is, Don't be a one-trick pony always doing the same thing in the same way. Have the attitude you need and the motivation you need to alter your approach to appeal more to the person doing the judging, whether she is your boss, your peer, or your direct report.

Mind-Set Eight: I Am a Teacher and a Student

I've struggled with the term "presentational skills coaching" since I began in practice. I've wrinkled my nose, so to speak, when clients have said, "I'm not a good presenter." But there are other statements that haven't been soul satisfying either:

"I'm not a good salesman."

"I'm not good at speaking."

"I'm not great at asserting."

"I'm weak at organizing."

"I'm reserved when I express myself."

Not even one client, however, has ever said, "I'm not a good teacher" or "My job doesn't include teaching." I think that's because clients do not think of themselves as teachers. So it's time for another mind-set: you should embrace the attitude that a large portion of your work life is the work of a teacher.

Why do I say that? Because every time you speak, you are evaluated the same way that students evaluate their teachers. Students think to themselves,

> Is she an organized lecturer?
>
> Is he an animated, good-natured person?
>
> Is he open to the views of the class?
>
> Is she easy to listen to? Can she keep me awake?
>
> Is his content interesting? Does he present it in an interesting way?

Begin to think to yourself, "When it's my chance to speak up at this meeting, I'm going to think of myself as a teacher who wants to make a great impression on my class."

Two years ago, we hired a consultant to join our staff. He had recently earned a master's in a communication program and was filled with some of the latest academic research out there. Most new staff members are cautious about speaking up too early in their career with a new firm. I'm aware of that and generally support the idea. Here's what I told him when he started. I said, "For the first few weeks here, when you attend a meeting, think of yourself as a student. Spend your time and effort listening and learning about the people and their views. But after two months or so, we're going to expect you to start 'teaching.' Bring up what you've learned at school. Bring up your views on internal issues even if they are based on instinct more than experience. Yes, be a student. But also stretch your teaching muscles."

He said, "It's a good way to look at it."

And that brings me to the second aspect of this mind-set. Many employees who receive feedback about the need to be a better listener are completely befuddled about it. They are always asking for examples, and they often argue with the examples when they get one. And, by the way, feedback givers are often loathe to give examples for just that reason. They get a big argument over it. They try to make the feedback giver realize that the example was a "one-off" or that there was a good reason for it. So, if your boss gives you an example, just say, "Oh." Now having gotten that little piece off my chest, I'm convinced that none of the people who are accused of poor listening would bristle so much at being told, "You need to come across as a good student." Even better and more to the point, "You don't come across as someone willing to learn." That is what all of us are asked to do when it comes to our listening behavior: we're being asked to try to learn something new.

How many times have you said something to a colleague like, "I just learned that Mike got the job," only to hear back, "Oh yeah. I knew that." Have you ever said, "I checked the numbers this morning and think we made an error yesterday," only to hear, "Oh yeah. I knew that."

Imagine the same scenario this way. You say, "I checked the numbers this morning and think we made an error yesterday." Your colleague says, "Tell me more." The simplest expressions of the desire to learn are so satisfying. I've said that it's the communicator's responsibility to make his or her idea compelling. And I'm also saying you don't need one or two seminars to practice this.

Mind-Set Nine: Gas or No Gas?

It was early in my career when I first heard someone describe a human being in terms of carbonation. The person who called our offices on behalf of a potential client said, "Jack is a salesman. He's a little over-carbonated." Since then I've heard the term "overcaffeinated" used to describe the same style. In Jack's case, let's just say he had a way with body language.

Humans typically use their hands when talking. Depending on our culture, we use them more or less. In America, an extremely common gesture is one we call the "basketball," which I mentioned in Chapter Six.

The basketball is an example of a gesture that's as right and normal and effective in the office or boardroom as it is at the backyard barbecue.

But Jack, it turns out, had been given some feedback years and years ago that he didn't move his hands enough when presenting, that he didn't appear sufficiently animated. He took the advice to heart and overcompensated. When he said, "I've been thinking . . . ," he touched his forehead. When he said, "The first reason is . . . ," he placed the forefinger on one hand in the palm of the other. When he said, "We're not communicating with any kind of flow," he moved his right hand back and forth across his chest as if he was directing traffic at a busy intersection. If he said, "It touched my heart," he touched his own chest. His gestures looked so contrived, so . . . well, overcarbonated. His boss said, "Get him to tone it down."

At first, Jack hadn't shown enough animation; using the carbonation metaphor, we would say that Jack had been flat, like a soft drink without bubbles. He then adjusted his behavior but overcompensated by showing too much animation; he became overcarbonated. Neither condition worked. Neither was effective in establishing and maintaining credibility. Your attitude in taking advice has to be, "I have to be careful about how much to adjust. Everyone is simply asking me to make a small adjustment."

Nowadays I have a professional colleague, Jeff Weiss at the Center for Corporate Innovation, who describes potential clients as needing to be "fanged" or "defanged." A client needs to be fanged if he needs to show more assertiveness and confidence. She needs defanging if she is showing too much assertiveness and too much confidence. Again, suggestions for change are best taken and best acted on in small ways. You will be bowled over to learn just how much a change in your credibility can be wrought with the smallest adjustments.

The first time I heard this issue talked about in an academic setting was when I was working on my master's degree at West Virginia University. Mike Burgoon explained that the relationship between *any* behavior you display and its ultimate impact on your credibility is curvilinear. "Curvilinear," a statistical notion, in this usage simply means that there's a point at which too much of a good thing is a bad thing. (Plain old "linear" means that the more there is of this, the more there is of that. Ad infinitum. The more money you make, the richer you'll be.) Suppose you hear that you need to speak up more at meetings. If you take that to heart and start doing exactly that, you will eventually reach a point of maximum credibility. You'll be contributing at a "just right" level. But what happens if you cannot stop yourself? Your credibility will start to drop as people say, "He can't shut up. He just wants to be heard. He loves to hear himself talk."

When you look at Figure 11.2, you'll see circles at the ends of the curve as well as circles close to the bell itself. The circles close to the bell represent the distance from "effective" that most observers see someone whom they feel is erring. In other words, they are saying, "try to make a *small* change in order to be more effective." They're saying a small change will put you in the bell—and that would be terrific. If they think you should delegate "a little more," they really mean, "a *little* more." They don't mean, "delegate everything." The circles at the ends of the curve symbolize making such a huge adjustment to your current behavior that the result of the change would be worse than the status quo. I don't care how pleasing a behavior might seem, you can take it to an extreme. And

Figure 11.2. How Much Is Too Much? The Credibility Curve.

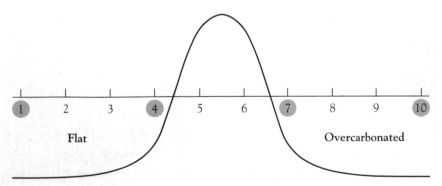

if you do, you will lose more credibility than you risk with the status quo. Burgoon illustrated this phenomenon with a curve similar to the one shown in Figure 11.2; we might call it the Credibility Curve.

Five years ago, I got together with a new client who was one of several candidates for a senior position at a law firm. He would be the *capo tutti de tutti,* the boss of bosses, the managing partner. I called him before we met face-to-face. I generally introduce myself on the phone before a first meeting.

Most of the time, my clients are reserved at that first call. They are ambiguous and ambivalent and confused and sometimes bewildered. They're wondering "what this is all about." But this guy sounded like he had been chomping at the bit for a consultant like me. "I can't wait." "You da man." "I'll be sitting at the feet of the master." Hmmmm.

When I arrived at the law offices a few days later, I was taken to his office. His assistant brought me some coffee in a paper cup. She told me he would arrive shortly. I waited maybe five minutes. When he came in, the apologies came in a torrent. OVERBOARD. When he saw I was drinking coffee in a paper cup, he was mortified. "Oh, no. That's not right. Marcie, you know better than that!" OVERBOARD. He said, "Let's get some real coffee. What would you like? Let's walk over to the kitchen." OVERBOARD. I said, "No, really. I like the coffee. I was in the Navy. I know bad coffee. This is just great. Marcie took good care of me."

"Nonsense," he said. "You come with me." OVERBOARD. In the kitchen he said, "OK. Tulley's, Seattle's Best, Starbucks?" "French Roast, Colombian, Indonesian . . ." I said, "Whatever's hot." But he just wouldn't or couldn't pick up on the fact that the brand and the taste weren't an issue for me. OVERBOARD.

We met a few times as the year progressed, and this notion of moderation was at the heart of our meetings. Everyone told him they liked his lower-key demeanor. He got the senior position. Now I'm not saying it was because of our work. He had the substance—the bona fides.

Four years later, though, they asked him to leave. He had reverted, little by little, to his original state. (As I mentioned earlier, I tell people that our consulting practice has a .700 batting average. Seven out of ten clients are perceived as much more credible. But some of them lose their edge. As when you're dieting, you have to be alert.)

No matter what the issue is—even, as in this case, politeness— every quality, taken to an extreme, has credibility consequences.

Mind-Set Ten: I Don't Need Myers-Briggs

Over nearly thirty years of consulting, I have heard of or experienced nearly every form of popular personality profiling offered by large corporations, including Personalysis, Myers-Briggs, DISC, and Enneagram.

The first time I saw a group go through the results of the testing was around 1980. In that case, everyone had taken the Myers-Briggs Type Indicator (MBTI). The types the MBTI refers to distinguish four variables. Those are extroversion/introversion, intuitiveness/analysis, thinking/feeling, and judging/perceiving. I remember participants tearing the perforated seal from the package. Everyone seemed excited about the prospect of finding out "who they really were." People said, "Yep. It's got me down cold." Others said things like, "I can't believe how accurate this is. I'm definitely introverted. I'm definitely a feeling kind of person." You would think they were poring over their horoscope.

The organizations that sponsor this kind of testing are typically not using it to place the right people in the right position. They use it as a way to improve communication among employees. The idea is that if someone working for me helps me understand her personality—the introverted side, let's say—I'll be able to work more effectively with her, and vice versa. How can we argue with that? Well, it's easy to argue with. Remember, the person who is judging you thinks you should be like her. An extroverted manager feels a greater connection with an extroverted subordinate. If a presentation must be made, the manager can trust the more outgoing subordinate to take her place if necessary. And the same goes for an introverted manager. He may feel that an introverted subordinate will come across as appropriately understated.

A client's boss is more intuitive than analytical on the MBTI. She announced it to her team when she took the position. My client asked me what that little bit of information would suggest. I told her, "When your boss asks you for your opinion on an issue, she wants to know your intuitive opinion. She'll respect that. Your opinion may have come as a result of months of analysis, but your answer should emerge right there on the spot."

The client said, "Why not just tell her I'm an MBTI analytical and prefer a little more time to think through my answer to questions like that?"

I told her, "Your boss may say 'OK. Thanks for letting me know.' But inside she'll think, 'I need to ask someone who is willing to give me his or her intuitive opinion. I can't wait for deeper analysis. I don't even know if I trust a deeper analysis.' "

Should you strive to come across in a way that clicks with your boss, or should you tell your boss that your personality is simply different from hers—and that you hope she'll appreciate that? I vote for "clicking."

There's something else to think about here. The MBTI in particular grew out of original research by Carl Jung. Jung's thesis was that all of us would benefit by stretching ourselves, that our need for self-fulfillment mandates an attempt to grow in areas where we're not a natural fit. On that basis alone, I strongly encourage my clients to try behavior that runs counter to their natural instinct. As the environmentalists say, "It's good for the bottle. It's good for the can." In this case, "It's good for your boss. It's good for you."

"Don't Take This Seminar" Number 3: Personal Styles. Don't take a personal styles seminar unless you are absolutely sure you'll learn about how to adjust your personal style.

Mind-Set Eleven:
The Individual Is the Unit of Analysis

At CDA, our client is the person we're working with, not the company that receives the invoice. As I've mentioned, we call the company the patron. A patron supports, protects, and champions, and we subscribe fully to that notion. I always say to the person I'm advising, "You are my client, and you're lucky enough to be working for an organization that wants you to do well."

A corollary to that philosophy is that at the end of the day, clients are responsible for their own productive and satisfying work life. If you say to yourself, "This whole situation would be better if I worked with other people" or "This whole situation would be better if people were on a different team," you are thinking globally (and not in a particularly wise manner) but not doing anything locally. So many times I've sat with a client who said, "Let me give you the background on some of this feedback I've received. You see, my boss had someone working for her before who she got along with really, really well. She's just got a 'thing' about me, and that's why I'm getting this feedback."

We've been called with this request: "Can you come in and do a team-building seminar? People here are not behaving as a team. There's a lot of conflict. People are holding side conversations at meetings, which shows disrespect for team members. Can you help us out?"

If I take the call, I say, "Let's start with sitting in on a team meeting. We'll get a sense of who is contributing in a positive way and who might be in need of some counsel." The caller might say, "But I don't want individuals to get advice. I want the whole team to get the message." To that I will respond, "Different people need different messages, so it makes sense to let every individual know what he or she can do to make things better."

The notion of a "better" team or a "more cohesive" team is an outcome of the group's doing things together and is not a great topic for a seminar. Did you know that most of the positive feedback given after an off-site team seminar is along the lines of "It was great just being able to talk to team members at dinner or over drinks and finding out that they worry about the same things I do"? You can create a team atmosphere by putting people near each other. You can create it by having them dress in corporate logo clothes. You can create it by having them play on the same softball team. But you can't create it by having them take a seminar on team building. The individual needs to know how he or she is helping or hurting.

> *"Don't Take This Seminar" Number 4: Team Building.* Take the seminar titled "How I Learned to Be a Better Team Member."

Mind-Set Twelve: I Am *Not* Being Manipulative

I have a peeve about individuals who excuse their unwillingness to learn about credibility by saying, "I would be manipulating people." It is getting to me more as I get older. My wife and I joke about certain peeves making my Top Ten list, and this one is dangerously close to qualifying.

Let's talk a little about manipulation by studying a personality trait known as Machiavellianism. I spent one year at the master's level studying what are known as "High Machs" and wrote my master's thesis about the phenomenon.

Machiavellianism describes a personality who loves to manipulate people for the sheer joy that comes from the activity. There's a test for the trait, which I've included as Appendix B. If you take it and score a low number, relax. No one is going to make you manipulative. If you score high, relax. There's not a darn thing you can do about it. No twelve-step programs.

Machiavellians, especially the really high-scoring ones (High Machs), have an uncanny ability to say the things that give others warm, fuzzy feelings. They can sell snow to people in Nome, Alaska. They have impeccable timing for the phrase that will change your mind. In short, if you did not study them, you would overlook a terrific opportunity to pick up tips.

They have really endearing qualities. For instance, they do not remember names. They think of people as targets. A high-scoring Mach might say, "Who was the tall guy at the meeting? I can't remember his name, but he might take a little extra persuasion before he comes around."

Here are a few of the tricks of their trade:

• They nod a lot. They know you will nod if they nod. And they do it when they're talking as well as when they are listening. It brings you "into the conversation."

• They look at you much more intensely than the average conversationalist, but not so much as to be intimidating. When someone says, "Bill Clinton makes everyone in a large audience feel like he's talking directly to them," bingo. I don't know President Clinton's test score. You think he's a High Mach? Naahhhh.

• They don't talk a lot. It's classic for a High Mach to wait until a group meeting is winding down, when he senses that people are tired and ready to go, to say, "Let me tell you what I think all of you are concluding." And then he will cast that conclusion in a way that benefits his agenda.

• They connect with you instantly. If a High Mach salesperson walks up to you in a clothing store, she will not say, "Can I help you?" Instead she'll say, "I've got a sweater over here that you will not be able to resist." What makes that so clever? They do not start a conversation with a question. They always start with a statement. Now that goes against everything you've ever been told, right? But it works. Ladies, if a guy walks up to you in a bar and says, "I was here last week, and the martinis were really special," fasten your seatbelt. This guy is no amateur. He knows it's not the quality of the line. It's that the line isn't a question.

I am not going to describe any more of their techniques because I refuse to help you become manipulative, and you don't want to anyway, right????

Mind-Set Thirteen: "It's All an Act" Is No Excuse

One way to talk yourself out of improving your perceived level of credibility is to say, "It's all an act. Even though I could pull it off, even though I know it would positively change the way I'm perceived, I'm not going to do it. It would be insincere."

Think about the things we do—the "acting" we do—to make sure our behavior is perceived the way we want it to be. Here are some examples:

Getting to work on time

Saying thank you for a gift you might not like

Dressing up for an employment interview

Praising a piece of art that you wouldn't give away

Sometimes a client will say to a consultant, "You're asking me to be someone I'm not." Maybe we've suggested that a CEO talk about something personal in a message to all the employees. First of all, even if it's a stretch, the ends are worth the means. Second, it's usually not such a stretch. My response to the "something I'm not" complaint is, "I'm asking you to be who you really are. The way you're presenting yourself threatens to come across as someone you're not."

I heard an anecdote once that really resonated with me. Those of you who are knowledgeable about acting, stage acting, may say I don't have the story entirely right, but here's how I heard it.

In 1979, Laurence Olivier and Dustin Hoffman did a movie together called *Marathon Man.* Hoffman's role included a scene where he's tortured by

Olivier's character. Hoffman considered himself a "method" actor. Olivier called himself a "technical" actor. Method acting requires the actor to "get into character." Getting into character means immersing oneself into the character's feelings so deeply that one almost becomes the character. Technical acting is as it sounds. That is, one thinks there's technique that will bring the scene to life. Olivier, as I heard it, believed there was a proper technique even for lifting an ashtray.

On the set, in talking about preparing for the torture scene, Hoffman said to Olivier, "I stayed up a couple of nights to get ready." Olivier said to Hoffman, "It's a lot easier to learn to act."

Boy, that says it all. You don't have to get into character to properly communicate your credibility. You can't depend on "just being yourself," nor can you rely on the advice of others who say, "Just be yourself." The self you are projecting might not be projecting credibility. Sounding like you have conviction may take a little acting on your part, but if it was good enough for Olivier, it's good enough for all of us.

Mind-Set Fourteen:
Gender Isn't the Huge Issue You Think It Is

Have you seen ads for seminars titled "Communication Skills for Women"? This drives me absolutely nuts.

> *"Don't Take This Seminar" Number 5: Communication Skills for Women.* I didn't write this book for men. I wrote it for everyone. No woman has ever said, "Your coaching only works for men."

There isn't enough legitimate data to support the belief that men and women need to learn communication skills unique to their gender. The idea sells books, but it doesn't hold up to scrutiny.

You could take a seminar on how to be alert to behaviors that women may, repeat *may*, do a little more or a little less than men.

Maybe women can talk with their friends a little longer than a man can about a problem without seeking an immediate solution. If you are a man, knowing that, maybe you'll be a little more patient.

I don't support a day-long seminar that claims, for instance, that men learned how to work in teams and women learned to work on their own. If you're expected to be a better team player, that's the coaching you need. Well, you can take the seminar if you need a day off from work.

Let's talk about the "may, repeat *may*" notion first. Dr. Deborah Tannen wrote the world's best book about women and communication. Armed with great data from her dissertation, she wrote *You Just Don't Understand: Women and Men in Conversation* (1991). The guy who wrote about Mars and Venus simply dumbed down Tannen's research.

In Tannen's book, she describes a behavior I *know* exists. Women may say or do things at the end of a sentence that unintentionally trivialize the content. Imagine yourself at a meeting. A conversation starts about a marketing plan. You, a woman, are asked for your opinion. You say, "I think we jumped into the whole thing without enough planning." A wonderful sentence. Well said. A sentence with the potential to change opinions. Can you hear yourself giggle after the sentence? It's as if you added, "Is it OK that I said that?"

The giggle protects you in case someone disagrees. Tannen says women do it more than men. But here's the thing: *any* sound at the end of sentence is troublesome. The only effective gesture is a nod as if to affirm your own view.

The end of a sentence carries the meaning *and* the emphasis. It must stand alone. True for men. True for women. True for Martians. True for Venetians. Women can take the same seminar as men to curb their appetite for giggling at the end of a thought. It doesn't need to be taught in a "Women Only" seminar. OK. I've had my say on this.

Well, not quite. Talking about Mars and Venus compels me to comment about "motivational speakers" or "motivational seminars." Sometimes people ask me if I'm a motivational speaker. I generally say, "I hope my message is motivating but I don't advertise it as motivational." Maybe I should.

As I completed the manuscript for *So Smart But . . .* , I saw an interview with Steve Salerno, the author of *SHAM* (2005). *SHAM* aims a spotlight on self-help gurus, and it's not a pretty sight. He exposes Laura Schlessinger, John Gray (the Mars and Venus guy), Phil McGraw, and Tony Robbins as fakirs.

My view of motivational speakers and radio gurus is a little different from Salerno's. I'm not opposed to any message that makes an audience member feel a little better. If someone leaves a seminar with a plastic card that says "I'm a good person" and pastes it on his computer screen, fine. I *don't* think that person should go to Successories and buy framed photos of sunsets that have little aphorisms like "The Sun Is Shining on Your Team" and post those in the conference room. Not wise for coming across credibly. They demonstrate a type of shallow approach to complex issues and will no doubt produce some looks from employees that convey thoughts like *I can't believe we're spending money on stuff like this*. And this is especially true if the "sponsor" of these messages encourages, maybe even requires, employees to use the language. That is, by far, the biggest mistake a guru can make: encouraging people to use certain words. It's not the words per se that leave the impression. It's the totality of the message and the way it's expressed.

In the late 1970s, I met an executive whose boss had brought a consultant and his seminar into the organization. Ultimately, stockholders brought a lawsuit against management for wasting company money on foolishness and for fostering, or sponsoring, a cult. And they won the lawsuit.

Here's the story. The company had spent a couple million on the consultant. His seminar title was "Leadership Skills for Executives." The problem was that the consultant encouraged the participants to use very specific language in their day-to-day conversation. The most annoying phrase was "I don't want compliance; I want conviction." If an employee didn't use the language, he or she was thought to be a slacker, thought to be someone who wouldn't drink the Kool-Aid. That's why employees thought it was a cult. (You may not have known this, but some employees have thought that Covey's *7 Habits of Effective People* had a religious, cultlike quality to it.)

The employees were supposed to say to the boss, "I want you to know that I'm not doing this because you're making me do it. I'm doing it because I want to." Woe betide the employee who didn't spout the right words.

Actually, if Salerno is annoyed with Tony Robbins's message, he might just as well be annoyed with a whole gaggle of evangelical ministers who have crossed the line from "preaching the word" to giving success advice. This guy Joel Osteen from Texas fits that description, as do Ed Young, also from Texas, and Joyce Meyers, who "preaches" in Nashville. When I was a kid in West Virginia, we used to see a preacher named Reverend Ike. Joel Osteen couldn't carry Reverend Ike's clerical collar. The preachers don't charge to listen to them, so in that sense, what they do is not egregious. They do sell tapes and books, however.

Now, having said that I think these people's messages are, well, questionable as to their long-term value, I nevertheless encourage my clients to watch them all to learn how to express themselves and how to come across as warm listeners. Evangelical preachers are very skilled at expressing themselves. The sentences are short. The pauses are dramatic. The analogies are clever. The words are simple. For goodness' sake, Phil McGraw is known for the phrase, "Get real." Salerno quotes him as saying, "And how's that workin' out for ya?" and "This is going to [gonna] be a changing day in your life" (2005, p. 65). I don't push colloquialisms on clients with all the final *g*'s left off, but you get the point. If a whole world of people is drawn to a style like this, you can't ignore it. McGraw is upbeat, his gestures are large, his face is full of expression, and when he's listening, he has that "Right now, you're the only one who matters" look on his face. I mentioned in Chapter Eight that my dad studied preachers of the "old time religion" for communication skills, including phrasing, pausing, and high-energy delivery. He was on to something.

Mind-Set Fifteen:
You Don't Have to Be Beautiful at Birth

The last bit of advice about attitude is intended for those of you who demand that people be born with credibility. Talk about bias. There is a bias in this country that if a person is not born with a skill, then he or she is not true or real. If one of your colleagues goes to a facilitated seminar to learn how to be a better presenter, don't remark, "He's just putting on a good face. He's a nervous wreck inside. He's not a natural presenter." If someone attends a seminar on adjusting to change, don't say, "He's acting so unnatural. He hates change. He's just doing what the seminar people told him to do." Even worse, if someone takes an interpersonal skills workshop and receives feedback that she needs to be more open to the views of others—and she takes that to heart—don't say, "She's no more open now than she ever was. She's just saying what they told her to say. It's a big put-on."

One current commercial for the U.S. Marines says, "Leaders are not born. They are made." That is so true. But some of you require leaders to pop out at birth. Give your colleagues a break. They really want to be better. They really want to be all they can be. They are busting their collective butts to take your organization to places it has never been. It's not right to put them down. It's not fair to belittle anyone's attempt to be better. All of us should say to them, "I appreciate the effort you're making—it means a lot."

Mind-Set Sixteen:
It's Okay to Be Deep and It's Okay to Be Superficial

This past week, a "patron" sent me an e-mail notifying me that a client he'd asked me to work with a month ago had since been fired. I called him to say that he should tear up the bill (which he refused to do), and he said something like this: "Allen, I should've realized that Brady's problems weren't superficial. His issues went much, much deeper." My knee-jerk reaction when we hung up was to be vaguely annoyed with the word *superficial*. I looked it up. *Superficial* means being concerned with only what is apparent or on the surface. One realizes immediately that all communication behavior, communication technique, is superficial, since by nature it's on the surface. It's what you see and what you hear. You hope that the words and actions reflect that which is deeper, but the receiver has to make the call about that. If you don't come across to your boss as strategic, and I give you advice about how to say something that comes across as strategic, we both hope it reflects your deeper understanding about strategy and that you only needed a way to reflect that deeper understanding through enhanced communication technique. When President Bush appears to us with an American flag pin, it's certainly superficial. But all of us hope that it reflects his deeper feelings for America. We make the call.

12

PARTING THOUGHTS

About twenty-five years ago, I took a call from the chairman of the litigation department at one of the largest law firms in Los Angeles. He said, "We've got five litigators, all partners, who have been described as arrogant. We've heard it from associates and partners, but, most important, we've been told about it by judges and in jury debriefs. Can you help? Can you give them some *really neat tips?*"

I said that it would be a privilege. "What do you consider a 'really neat tip'?" I asked him. "If a judge feels like an attorney won't make the effort to look at him, would that be a really neat tip or just an average tip?"

The caller chuckled and said that most attorneys would be annoyed to hear a consultant talk about eye contact. "You'll have to come up with the really neat psychological tips," he said.

We began to talk about the consulting arrangement. I asked if "the Five" had been given the heads up that I would be calling to arrange meetings. "No. No one has the guts to bring it up." He said that the firm was going to have a partners' meeting at a local resort. He thought that 350 of their attorneys would be attending to listen to a variety of speakers. I would be one of them. I would be billed as a speaker on communication skills for attorneys. Before my session, he would point the Five out. I could begin my talk and, as I walked around, call on one or two of them as if at random. I could just hear myself saying, "Uh . . . you, sir. What would you say if I told you that everyone thinks you're arrogant?"

I could have used the money—this call came at the very start of our practice—but I turned down the engagement. I told the caller that when the firm was ready to give the attorneys some feedback about their style, it would be a privilege to be asked to advise them on how to communicate more effectively.

This story points out so many of the wonderfully interesting things about communication, about the consulting life, and about communication consulting. Communication separates us from every other form of life. The consulting life brings you in front of some of the world's most interesting people. Communication consulting allows you to help someone, and what could be better than that?

And that is why I am writing this book. I, and many others who have worked at CDA for thirty years, have been asked to write down our secrets, our formulas, and our insights—our really neat tips. We've put them in binders. We've put them on our website. We've put them in newsletters. We've written about them in articles. But we've never written a book. Over the years, I've hesitated to write one because I didn't know if the power of a consulting suggestion could "translate." Would the insights laid out in a book help readers the way face-to-face contact has the potential to help a client? As it turned out, I've loved writing *So Smart But . . .* , and now I am more confident about the power of this message, this message about personal credibility, to make a real difference in your life.

Appendix A

ESSESSNET QUESTION SETS

*Communication: Your Credibility as Judged
by Your Clarity Across a Variety of Settings*

1. Do I openly communicate what I'm thinking and feeling?

2. In my communication, do I make sure all necessary parties are included?

3. Does my verbal communication match my nonverbal communication?

4. Do I get to the point and communicate in a concise manner?

5. When using e-mail, do I provide pertinent information in a clear and organized manner?

6. Do I express myself at appropriate times in appropriate places?

7. Do I share my opinions effectively in meetings and groups?

8. Do I listen well and respond accordingly?

9. In conversation, do I stay on topic as opposed to drifting and becoming tangential?

10. Do I answer questions directly and concisely?

11. Do I make a conscious effort to adapt my message to the audience?

12. Am I generally assertive in my communication, as opposed to being either passive or aggressive?

Conflict Management: Your Credibility as Demonstrated
by Your Behavior During Conflict Situations

1. Do I take responsibility and ownership by acknowledging the part I've played in the conflict?

2. Do I express my thoughts and feelings appropriately in conflict situations?

3. In a conflict, do I focus on the issue(s) rather than the person or people involved?

4. Do I seem to have a comprehensive understanding of the issues in a conflict situation?

5. Am I composed and professional during times of disagreement?

6. In a conflict, do I listen to all parties involved and treat everyone fairly and equally?

7. In times of disagreement, do I strike you as open and willing to consider other perspectives and opinions?

8. Do I treat you with respect, as opposed to having a condescending quality during conflict situations?

9. Do I recognize and validate points of view that differ from mine?

10. In resolving conflict, do I suspend judgment until I know all the facts?

11. In resolving conflict, do I spend time looking for solutions and next steps as opposed to assigning blame or punishment?

12. After a conflict situation has been resolved, do I maintain appropriate professionalism and decorum as opposed to holding grudges?

Constructive Criticism: Your Credibility as
Judged by Your Ability to Accept Criticism

1. Do I use criticism as a means of growth for you and/or others?

2. Do I provide strengths and weaknesses when offering constructive criticism?

3. Do I solicit input from you and others when offering constructive criticism?

4. Do I provide criticism in a timely manner?

5. Do I offer constructive criticism in appropriate places?

6. Am I straightforward when offering criticism providing concrete, practical examples?

7. When discussing constructive criticism, do I encourage solutions and ideas for improvement?

8. Do I try to encourage agreement on action steps?

9. Do I seem to put effort into following up after I either receive or deliver constructive criticism?

10. Do I seek feedback regularly on my performance?

11. Do I react professionally when I receive constructive criticism?

12. Do I express my gratitude for your efforts in providing me feedback?

Credibility: The Flagship Questionnaire

1. Do I communicate in a clear and concise manner?

2. When you are talking, do I appear to be listening?

3. Do I come across as having a broad, strategic view of the business?

4. Do I come across as upbeat and friendly?

5. Would you describe me as decisive, someone who pushes forward and moves things along?

6. Do I treat you as an equal as opposed to having a condescending quality?

7. Do I strike you as being open-minded?

8. When I am asked a question, do I get to the point as opposed to giving a long-winded, complex answer?

9. Do I handle stress well and come across as composed in high-pressure situations?

10. Do I come across as inviting or at least accepting of constructive criticism as opposed to being defensive?

11. Does my opinion come across as value-added on topics for which I am supposed to have expertise?

12. Do I come across as a problem-solver and create a solution-oriented environment?

Decision Making: Your Credibility as
Demonstrated by Opportunities for Decision Making

1. Would you describe me as decisive, someone who pushes forward and moves things along?

2. Do I share my opinion and come across as value-added on items for which I am supposed to have expertise?

3. Do I appear comfortable when making decisions?

4. Are my decisions well thought out?

5. Do I involve you and the team in the decision-making process?

6. Do my decisions seem appropriate and topical as opposed to self-serving or having a "hidden agenda"?

7. Am I open to the input of others before making a decision?

8. Do I show support for the decisions that my team and I make?

9. Do I suggest action steps and follow up on decisions?

10. Do I challenge conventional thinking and provide insightful perspectives during the decision-making process?

11. Do I give everyone a chance to be heard during the decision-making process?

12. Do I act in a collaborative fashion during the decision-making process?

Downward Communication:
Your Credibility as Judged by Direct Reports

1. Do I provide proper direction and guidance in a clear, timely manner?

2. Do I provide you with the basics necessary to accomplish your job?

3. Do I make an effort to see that people aren't overworked?

4. Do I delegate work and assign tasks appropriately?

5. Do I treat everyone fairly and equally?

6. Do I seek your input and feedback?

7. Do I seem genuinely interested in what you have to say?

8. Do I shoot straight with you?

9. When working together, am I more likely to suspend judgment and hear you out rather than jump to conclusions?

10. Do I keep you well informed and updated?

11. Do I make myself available?

12. Do I show appreciation for your work and the work of others?

Interpersonal Relationships: Your Credibility
as Demonstrated by Your Ability to Connect with Others

1. Do I come across as upbeat and friendly?

2. Do I make an effort to relate well to others?

3. Am I polite and considerate demonstrating basic cordiality?

4. Am I trustworthy and dependable?

5. Do I participate in the social atmosphere inside and/or outside the workplace?

6. Do I make you feel included when we're together?

7. Do I generally come across as optimistic and positive?

8. Do I collaborate well with others using a cooperative working style?

9. When you are talking, do I appear to be listening?

10. Do I help to create a relatively stress-free environment?

11. Do I seem flexible and able to go with the flow?

12. Would you describe me as a team player?

Interviewer Skills: Your Credibility as Seen
by an Interviewee in a Recent Interview

1. Did I present our organization in a professional manner?
2. Did I seem to listen to your responses?
3. Did I provide enough detail around what we do and the way we do it?
4. Did I ask questions clearly?
5. Did I come across as approachable?
6. Did I clearly communicate our organizational needs and how you may fit into that objective?
7. Did I ask a good mix of questions that solicited the value you could provide our organization?
8. Did I create a relaxed and unthreatening environment?
9. Did I seem honest and trustworthy with the information I was providing you?
10. Did I seem well versed in what we are looking for?
11. Did I allow you enough time to share and present yourself as opposed to monopolizing the conversation?
12. Did I ask follow-up questions and seek feedback from you around clarification or additional information?

Interviewing Skills: Your Credibility as Seen
by an Interviewer When You Interviewed for a Position

1. Did I present myself in a professional manner?
2. Did I seem to listen to your questions and respond appropriately?
3. Did I provide enough detail about my background and expertise?
4. Was I answering your questions in a clear and direct manner?
5. Did I come across as approachable and easy to work with?

6. Did the value I bring to the table seem applicable to the position and your organization?

7. Did I maintain composure and minimize any anxiety I may have been experiencing?

8. Did I come across as prepared and ready for the interview?

9. Did I seem honest and trustworthy?

10. Was I able to balance my presentation with both a broad, strategic view and a detailed level of responses?

11. Did I show an appropriate amount of interest and desire?

12. Was I open to your input and any suggestions you may have provided?

*Leadership: Your Credibility as Judged
by Your Opportunities to Lead*

1. Do I come across as having a broad, strategic view?

2. Do others look to me as an opinion leader?

3. Do I demonstrate a strong work ethic?

4. Do I provide guidance and assistance to others around me?

5. Am I respectful of others?

6. Do I come across as inspiring and motivating?

7. Do I care about the development and success of the organization, as well as the people within the organization?

8. Do I provide people with the appropriate amount of support as opposed to being distant or micromanaging?

9. Do you think of me as someone who recognizes and rewards good performance?

10. Do my motives for supporting an idea seem open and honest as opposed to having a "hidden agenda"?

11. Do I treat everyone fairly and equally?

12. Am I clear in communicating my expectations and our corporate goals?

Management Skills: Your Credibility
as Judged by Your Ability to Manage

1. Do I ensure that people are on task and deadlines are being met?

2. Do I organize our resources appropriately and clearly communicate priorities?

3. Do I provide enough direction and guidance?

4. Do I treat you with respect?

5. Do I handle stress well and come across with composure and professionalism?

6. Am I open and available for others to provide me input and feedback?

7. Do I recognize and validate others' opinions and ideas?

8. Am I reliable and dependable in getting things done?

9. Do I demonstrate value-added expertise in the area that I manage?

10. Do I provide people with the appropriate amount of support as opposed to being distant or micromanaging?

11. Do I communicate upward and downward appropriately?

12. Do I recognize and reward good performance?

Presentation Skills: Your Credibility as
Demonstrated Through Presentation Opportunities

1. Do I present in a clear and concise manner?

2. Do I come across as having a broad, strategic view of the subject?

3. Do I come across as engaging and interesting?

4. When I'm asked a question, do I get to the point as opposed to giving a long-winded, complex answer?

5. Do I easily gain your attention?

6. Do I use effective evidence to prove my points?

7. Does my presentation seem organized and easily understood?

8. Do I handle visual aids well?

9. Do I use nonverbal communication (i.e., eye contact, hand gestures, etc.) to my advantage?

10. Do I appear to care about my subject?

11. Do I manage my nervousness well and control any anxiety I may have?

12. Do I facilitate audience participation comfortably?

Problem Solving: Your Credibility
as Demonstrated by Your Problem Solving

1. Do I exhibit a collaborative mind-set when solving problems?

2. Do I make an effort to involve others in the problem-solving process?

3. Do I push for a commitment to action when solving problems?

4. Do I first try to understand the situation and all perspectives involved as opposed to jumping the gun and making a quick decision?

5. Am I able to explain the nature of a problem and its solutions with the appropriate level of detail and concern?

6. Am I equally capable of laying out a strategy as I am of discussing tactical action?

7. In the problem-solving process, do I treat you with respect as opposed to having a condescending or demeaning quality?

8. When we're working together, am I more likely to suspend judgment and hear you out as opposed to jumping to conclusions?

9. When I'm involved in a search for solutions with my team, do I recognize new ideas and validate other opinions?

10. Do my motives for supporting an idea seem open and honest as opposed to having a "hidden agenda"?

11. Am I fact based as opposed to having a reputation for exaggerating?

12. When necessary, am I able to make a persuasive argument and use effective evidence to prove my points?

Strategic Thinking: Your Credibility as Demonstrated by Your Strategic Mind-Set

1. Do I look to capture and understand the "big picture"?

2. Do I show that the work environment is fluid and adapt with flexibility?

3. Do I seem to plan a couple of steps ahead and try to anticipate what is around the corner?

4. Do I demonstrate composure and professionalism when the unexpected occurs?

5. Do I come up with original ideas and contribute to accomplishing our strategy?

6. Am I wise in the battles I choose to fight?

7. Would you describe me as forward-looking and visionary?

8. Am I constantly looking for new challenges, as opposed to resting on old glories?

9. Do I tap diverse points of view as opposed to staying within my own comfort zone?

10. Do I consider hypothetical situations by engaging in those types of discussion?

11. Do I lay out my views in a logical manner?

12. Am I able to see the consequences of the actions I propose?

Team Communication: Your Credibility as Judged by Team Members

1. Do I share information openly and honestly with my team members?

2. Do I make efforts to check in and update other team members?

3. Do I make others feel as though they are integral parts of the team?

4. Do I listen to the input of my fellow team members?

5. Do I respond appropriately to other team members' ideas and suggestions?

6. Do I treat others with respect?

7. Does my opinion come across as value-added on items for which I am supposed to have expertise?

8. Do I seem committed to our team goals?

9. When working together, am I more likely to suspend judgment and hear you out rather than jump to conclusions?

10. Have I contributed to a healthy team atmosphere?

11. Do I shoot straight with all team members?

12. Does our team operate with the appropriate amount of action items, meetings, and follow-ups?

*Team Player: Your Credibility as
a Motivator as Judged by Your Team*

1. Do I "hold my own" on the team and do my job accurately and timely?

2. Do I foster a cohesive and collaborative atmosphere?

3. Am I a source of motivation for the rest of my team, encouraging other team members?

4. Do I search for people with different points of view and expertise that create a well-rounded perspective?

5. Do I periodically check to see that everyone is "on the same page"?

6. Do I challenge the status quo and pose things in "a different light" to spark thought from others?

7. Do I deal with change in a productive manner?

8. Do I recognize and acknowledge the value others provide?

9. Do I appear to want to be part of a team?

10. Do I show respect for team decisions, even if I may not agree with them?

11. Do I demonstrate good listening behavior at team meetings?

12. Do I engage with people socially as to create a bond with team members?

Technical Ability: Your Credibility as
Demonstrated by Your Technical Ability

1. Do I come across as competent in my tasks?

2. Do I accomplish items accurately and timely?

3. Do I sufficiently understand my role and what I am supposed to produce?

4. Do I share my professional expertise with those around me?

5. Do I bring new ideas and fresh thinking to my position?

6. Does my opinion come across as value-added on topics for which I'm supposed to have expertise?

7. Do I demonstrate sufficient ability and technical background?

8. Do I appear to want to learn about a variety of technical topics that would make me more effective?

9. Does my technical experience overshadow my ability to demonstrate the broader business perspective?

10. Am I considered a "thought partner" in my particular business unit?

11. Do I seem to understand our industry?

12. Do I offer enough direction and guidance?

Upward Communication: Your Credibility
as Judged by Those Senior to You

1. Do I communicate in a clear and concise manner?

2. When you are talking, do I appear to be listening?

3. Do I come across as composed in high-pressure situations?

4. Do I provide you with what you need to get the job done?

5. Do I seem committed to our team goals?

6. Do I come across as inviting or at least accepting of constructive criticism?

7. Do I demonstrate the confidence and conviction needed to be an effective leader?

8. Do I come across as having a broad, strategic view of the business?

9. Do I have the style and business etiquette to move up in the organization?

10. Am I respectful of others?

11. When I'm asked a question, do I get to the point as opposed to giving a long-winded, complex answer?

12. Am I able to connect the day-to-day operations with the overall organizational strategy?

Appendix B

THE TEST FOR MACHIAVELLIANISM

Indicate the degree to which you agree with the statements below by circling your response, using the following 1–7 scale: 1 = strongly agree; 2 = agree; 3 = slightly agree; 4 = neither agree nor disagree; 5 = slightly disagree; 6 = disagree; 7 = strongly disagree. Instructions for scoring appear at the end of the test.

Work quickly and record your first impression.

1. Never tell anyone the real reason you did something unless it is useful to do so.   1 2 3 4 5 6 7
2. The best way to handle people is to tell them what they want to hear.   1 2 3 4 5 6 7
3. One should take action only when sure it is morally right.   1 2 3 4 5 6 7
4. Most people are basically good and kind.   1 2 3 4 5 6 7
5. It is safest to assume that all people have a vicious streak and that it will come out when they are given a chance.   1 2 3 4 5 6 7
6. Honesty is the best policy in all cases.   1 2 3 4 5 6 7
7. There is no excuse for lying to someone else.   1 2 3 4 5 6 7
8. Generally speaking, people won't work hard unless they're forced to do so.   1 2 3 4 5 6 7
9. All in all, it is better to be humble and honest than important and dishonest.   1 2 3 4 5 6 7
10. When you ask someone to do something for you, it is best to give the real reasons for wanting it rather than giving reasons that might carry more weight.   1 2 3 4 5 6 7

11. Most people who get ahead in the world lead clean, moral lives.   1 2 3 4 5 6 7

12. Anyone who completely trusts anyone else is asking for trouble.   1 2 3 4 5 6 7

13. The biggest difference between most criminals and other people is that criminals are stupid enough to get caught.   1 2 3 4 5 6 7

14. Most people are brave.   1 2 3 4 5 6 7

15. It is wise to flatter important people.   1 2 3 4 5 6 7

16. It is possible to be good in all respects.   1 2 3 4 5 6 7

17. P. T. Barnum was very wrong when he said there's a sucker born every minute.   1 2 3 4 5 6 7

18. It is hard to get ahead without cutting corners here and there.   1 2 3 4 5 6 7

19. People suffering from incurable diseases should have the choice to be put painlessly to death.   1 2 3 4 5 6 7

20. Most people forget more easily the death of their father than the loss of their property.   1 2 3 4 5 6 7

Scoring

Reverse your score for questions 1, 2, 5, 8, 12, 13, 15, 16, 18, 19, and 20. In other words, if for these questions you circled 1, give yourself a 7. If you circled 2, give yourself a 6, and so on.

Total your scores. If your total score is over 112, seek a job in politics. By that I mean, you've got the ability to separate yourself from the passions of the topic at hand and concentrate on what you need to do to get people to support your point of view.

References

Applebaum, R. L., & Anatol, K. W. (1973). Dimensions of source credibility: A test for reproductivity. *Speech Monographs, 40,* 230–237.

Bandhuim, E. S., & Davis, M. K. (1972). Scales for the measurement of ethos: Another attempt. *Speech Monographs, 39,* 296–301.

Baker, R. (2006). Talking it up. *The New York Review of Books, 53*(8), 4–6.

Berlo, D. K., Lemert, J. B., & Mertz, R. J. (1971). Dimensions for evaluating the acceptability of message sources. *Public Opinion Quarterly, 33,* 563–576.

Burgoon, M., Hunsaker, F. G., & Dawson, E. J. (1994). *Human communication.* Thousand Oaks, CA: Sage.

Canfield, J. (1993). *Chicken soup for the soul.* Deerfield Beach, FL: Health Communications.

Falcione, R. L. (1974). The factor structure of source credibility scales for immediate supervisors in an organizational context. *Central States Speech Journal, 25,* 63–66.

Himsel, D. (2003). *Leadership Sopranos style.* Chicago: Kaplan Publishing.

Klein, J. (2006). *Politics lost.* New York: Doubleday.

McCroskey, J. C. (1966). Scales for the measurement of ethos. *Speech Monographs, 33,* 65–72.

McCroskey, J. C., Hamilton, P. R., & Weiner, A. N. (1973). The effect of interaction behavior on source credibility, homophily, and interpersonal attraction. *Human Communication Research, 1,* 42–52.

McCroskey, J. C., & Jensen, T. A. (1975). Image of mass media news sources. *Journal of Broadcasting, 19,* 169–180.

McCroskey, J. C., & Teven, J. J. (1999). Goodwill: A reexamination of the construct and its measurement. *Communication Monographs, 66–91.*

McCroskey, J. C., & Young, T. J. (1981). Ethos and credibility: The construct and its measurement after three decades. *Central States Speech Journal, 32,* 24–34.

McKechnie, J. L. (Ed.). (1983). *Webster's new twentieth century dictionary of the English language, unabridged* (2nd ed.). New York: Simon & Schuster.

Rogers, E. M., with Shoemaker, F. F. (1971). *Communication of innovations: A cross-cultural approach.* London: Collier-MacMillan.

Salerno, S. (2005). *SHAM.* New York: Random House.

Tannen, D. (1991). *You just don't understand: Women and men in conversation.* New York: Ballantine.

Toulmin, S. (1958). *Uses of argument.* New York: Cambridge University Press.

Acknowledgments

To my wife, Carol Weiner. When I told her thirty years ago that I wanted to be a communication consultant, she did not faint. She put on a good face. She's had to suffer through a thousand comments like, "It must be so interesting being married to a communication consultant." And yes, she is the one who smiles and says to me, "Save your communication techniques for your clients."

To all university communication studies scholars who've dedicated years to rigorous behavioral studies. You've set the table for consultants like me. West Virginia University and the University of Southern California, a public and a private institution respectively, are two of the very best. Moms and dads, when your teenager tells you he or she wants to study communication, be supportive. And tell them to call me for advice.

To the professional colleagues who for thirty years have referred me to their clients. I know the chance you take in saying, "I'm going to have Allen Weiner call you. He can make a contribution." That list includes but isn't limited to Marc Gamson of Media and Thompson, Jeff Weiss of the Center for Corporate Innovation, and Brad Spencer of Spencer, Shenk, Capers.

To Malcolm Kushner, my agent. He's the model for the expression "keepin' it real." He knows BS when he hears it, and he's not shy in letting me know.

To Marie Lopez, my executive assistant for eight years. My clients hear her voice before mine. You can guess how vulnerable a firm like ours is to someone's saying, "Hey, for a communication consultancy, you don't communicate very well." Because of Marie, that doesn't happen. When it appeared that Marie might leave last year, a hundred people must have said, "Allen, what in the world are you going to do?" Relax. She's staying.

To CDA's consultants, who have meant so much to our success since the first one, John Waldron. Their hard work brought honor and grace to CDA. They've all started successful firms of their own.

To my sisters, Marsha and Harriet. Everyone needs a sister or two who make you feel that you can do anything and end every phone call with, "I love you."

To Alan Wohl of Wohl and Company. He's a great accountant, and I'm proud to be among the clients he considers a friend. I'm in some pretty august company.

To our son, Matt. He's going to need a job when school's over in 2008. I'd love to pull some strings. I told him to take any job he could find this summer. He said, "You do what you love to do, so why shouldn't I?" Hoist on my own petard.

To my clients. I also told Matt to think about a career in which you have the chance to build a reputation with our country's most talented professionals, and all of you are most certainly that. When you call, I feel like your cabinet officer for communication and credibility issues. I'm so flattered by your decision to have me work with you.

To my editors at Jossey-Bass, without whom I would never have had a book. Now I know why authors dedicate books to their editors.

To Lloyd Loomis of Lewis, Brisbois, Bisgaard and Smith in Los Angeles who cowrote Chapter Nine. He was gracious with his time and effort. He loves his work, and it shows.

To the extraordinary people of West Virginia and especially its public school teachers and coal miners. I include the miners because your fathers and grandfathers shopped at my dad's store on Summers Street in Charleston from 1930 until he closed in 1961. He allowed me to sit around the "cracker barrel" when they came to buy wedding suits or Sunday-go-to-meeting clothes and talk politics. You were the first to make me realize that wisdom isn't common sense—it makes sense. And although my official biography mentions outside interests such as books and music, my passionate interest is in the good fortune of West (By God) Virginia and the WVU Mountaineers.

—*Allen Weiner*

The Author

ALLEN WEINER is the cofounder and managing director of Communication Development Associates, Inc., in Woodland Hills, California, which celebrated its thirtieth anniversary in March 2006. Allen serves as adviser to senior management on a variety of issues related to human communication. His external responsibilities include on-site delivery of seminars and individualized coaching.

Allen completed his bachelor's and master's degrees in speech communication at West Virginia University. He received his Ph.D. in communication studies in 1976 from the Annenberg School of Communication at the University of Southern California.

His research interests were and remain persuasion, personal influence, and interpersonal credibility. Allen spends his free time in rare bookstores, taking bass guitar lessons, and traveling with his family. *So Smart But . . .* is his first book.

Allen is married to Carol Weiner and has a twenty-year-old son, Matt, who attends George Washington University.